Estate Planning in Georgia

— Keeping It in the Family —

Estate Planning in Georgia

— Keeping It in the Family —

The Smart Way to Leave Assets to Your Family
and Protect It from Disability, Taxes, Bad
Marriages, and Irresponsibility

Jeffrey I. Fouts, Esq.

ISBN: 978-1-59571-962-1

Designed and published by
Word Association Publishers
205 Fifth Avenue
Tarentum, Pennsylvania 15084

www.wordassociation.com
1.800.827.7903

Dedication

This book is dedicated to my wife, Laura, who has been my loving companion for decades.

I also dedicate the book to the valuable mentors and counselors I've had over the years; they know who they are.

Jeffrey I. Fouts, Esq.

Warning and Disclaimer

The laws, rules, and regulations pertaining to estate planning are highly complex and constantly changing. Furthermore, information can become outdated overnight by changes made by the IRS, Congress, the State of Georgia, or court cases that change legal interpretations and policies.

This book is intended to provide a general, broad overview regarding estate planning; it is in no way a substitute for the advice of a qualified, experienced, estate planning attorney who will look into your specific facts and circumstances and give advice based on that.

Neither the author nor the publisher is here engaged in the rendering of legal, accounting, or other professional services. The author and the publisher specifically disclaim any responsibility for any liability, loss, or risk (personal, financial, or otherwise) that may be claimed or incurred as a consequence, directly or indirectly, of the use or application of any of the contents of this book.

In other words, don't use this book as a self-help guide. Seek the advice of an experienced estate planning attorney.

Table of Contents

Foreword 13

Estate Planning Is Life Planning, Not Just Death Planning 15

What's the Real Purpose of Estate Planning? 19

Most People Haven't Done *Any* Estate Planning! 23

I'm Not Rich! I Don't Have an "Estate!" 27

I Don't Care What Happens to My Stuff (or Family) after I Die—
I'm *Not* Planning 31

Georgia Has an Estate Plan for You if You Don't Have One
Yourself 33

It's Not about Legal Documents—It's about Protecting Your
Family 35

Protecting Your Children's Inheritance from Creditors,
Bankruptcy, Divorce, or Costs of Your Illnesses 37

History of Estate Planning 39

Protecting from the Grave—How to Give Love and Wisdom
after You're Gone 43

The Goals of Estate Planning 45

No Surprises for Your Family 47

Making Sure You Don't Accidentally Disinherit Your
Children 49

Not Accidentally Leaving Your Home to Just One Child . 51

Talking Frankly about Your Values with Your Children 53

Managing Joint Tenancy, Joint Accounts, and Other Types of
Joint Ownership 57

Avoiding Family Conflicts 63

Making Sure Your Inheritances Aren't Squandered 67

Getting a Handle on the Different Estate Planning
    Documents 71

Understanding the Changing Definitions of "Family" 73

Striking Equality with Your Benefactors' Inheritances .. 75

Making Sure a Grandchild's Bequest Is Not Wasted by a
    Child 79

Avoiding Problems Caused by Leaving Real Estate Jointly to
    Children 83

Equalizing Bequests with Differing Levels of Debt 87

Keeping Children from Wasting Inheritances 89

Having Quality Power of Attorney Documents 91

Making Sure Your Children Receive Their Inheritances if
    Your Spouse Remarries 95

Making Sure Children Don't Receive Inheritances at Too
    Young an Age 97

Making Sure Life Insurance Proceeds Are Handled
    Properly 99

Not Giving Too Much Too Soon to Children 101

Naming Guardians for Minor Children 103

Understanding Adult Guardianship and
    Conservatorship 107

Understanding Alternatives to Adult Guardianship and
    Conservatorship 113

Understanding the Importance of Estate Planning 117

Understanding Probate: A Time-Consuming, Stressful Job at the Worst Possible Time 125

Using the Right Tools for the Right Job 127

Understanding the Different Kinds of Wills 131

Understanding the Different Parts of a Will 133

Understanding that a Will is a Tool 135

Avoiding Challenges to Your Will 147

Understanding Trusts 155

Making Sure Your Trust Does What You Want It To 159

Getting in the Habit of Reviewing Your Will 165

Changing Your Will after You Change Your Mind 167

Seeing a Living Trust as a Tool 171

Protecting Assets from Nursing Home Expenses 175

Learning the Facts of Medicaid 179

Understanding the Importance of Long-Term Care Insurance: Don't Turn Up Your Nose Just Yet! 183

Medicade Planning 187

Glossary 193

Additional Reading 209

About the Author 211

Foreword

If you are thinking about estate planning, it probably means two things: you have some assets (and it doesn't matter whether they are a little or a lot, and you have one or more people to whom you'd like to leave it to.

Every day, people who are smart in every other respect go around giving little if any thought to the great need they have for quality estate planning. They think they have all the time in the world to plan. Truth be told, they put more thought into planning their vacations than they do planning how to properly deal with their most valued possessions and those they love.

And then there are many who have done some estate planning and think what they've done will accomplish their goals, but sadly, this is often not the case.

My hope is that this book will cause you to realize the importance of estate planning and get you thinking about it in a radically different manner.

If this book does that, it will have accomplished its goal.

Sincerely,

Jeffrey I. Fouts
Attorney at Law

Estate Planning Is Life Planning, Not Just Death Planning

> "The lines have fallen for me in pleasant places;
> indeed, I have a beautiful inheritance."
>
> —Psalm 16:6 (Holman Christian Standard Bible)

Estate planning has a funny reputation. Most people think of it solely as "death" planning—who will get their assets after they die?

While estate planning is certainly about deciding who you will leave your assets to, it should be, and it can be, much more than that. It should be called "life" planning, because modern estate planning is about planning for what happens to you *during* your life as well as what happens to your surviving spouse and your children and grandchildren after you die.

Thinking Ahead:
The Lives of Those You Love and Will Leave Behind

Modern estate planning looks into the future not just to your death but also to the time of your life before you die and at many years after you die. It looks at how you and your spouse will manage each other in case of disability and how, once you die, your spouse will best be cared for.

Once both spouses have passed away, modern estate planning looks even deeper into the future. It deals with how your assets should best be given to your children and perhaps your grandchildren in this sense: proper estate planning will look at the personalities, capabilities, strengths, and weaknesses of not only your children and their spouses but also at your wishes for your grandchildren.

Solid estate planning will take into consideration potential threats to your, your spouse's, your children's and your grandchildren's wellbeing. It will weigh the risks and utilize time-tested techniques to deal with threats to your assets and to your family.

Generic Planning Documents Just Won't Do

Estate planning is so much more than simply pulling a form off the Internet or filling out a do-it-yourself document. These are flimsy tools when it comes to estate planning, and using them and then relying on them to give you a sense of security may give you a sense of security, but it will be a false sense of security. You could be setting yourself and others up for major heartache when it comes time for these cookie-cutter, noncustomized documents to actually perform.

You could conceivably lose so much more in time, money, and peace of mind by any attempt to save a few dollars with standard, generic wills and trust forms. What's worse, after your death, you could leave your spouse, children—all of those you want to help—with avoidable losses and great messes to clean up. It's the same as an army using faulty armor plating; soldiers may feel secure behind it, but they'll be terribly harmed when it fails to do what it's supposed to do.

The Mortality Rate is Terribly High

Why do people put off planning? I want to tell you something very personal—I'm going to die. I just don't know when. You're going to die as well. You've lived your life trying to be responsible, trying to take care of your obligations, and now is not the time to stop. People you love are counting on you.

What's the Real Purpose of Estate Planning?

> "Planning is bringing the future into the present so that you can do something about it now."
>
> —Alan Lekein

Estate planning isn't about money; it's about protecting your loved ones, and your money just happens to be a big way that you can protect them.

Money Is a *Part* of the Plan—Family Is the Main Part

You must look forward in time, but not just to your death. You need to think about what will happen when bad health hits you. But you also need to think about how your spouse will live after you're gone. You need to think about how your children will handle the inheritances (perhaps a lump sum of money or a valuable asset) you'll leave them.

The goal here is not simply come up with a list of your assets and divide them up between your beneficiaries and be done with it;

the goal is to leave your assets of all types to them in such a way that it will actually benefit them rather than harm them.

Building Stronger Families

Money and things can actually weaken families. Inheritances given in lump sums can have a bad effect on most people. That sounds pretty dire, but many people—and we all know some—don't have the discipline to manage money, even a seemingly small amount of it in such a way that it benefits them in the longer term.

If your goal is to strengthen your family and build stronger family bonds, you'll want to take great care in how you leave your money and things to your family to actually strengthen those bonds.

Proverbs 20:21 says, "An inheritance gained hastily in the beginning will not be blessed in the end" (ESV). Your goal should be to prevent any of those who receive an inheritance from you from developing a lottery winner's mindset. You should, and can, take steps to ensure that they will use your hard-earned money or asset to better themselves over the *long* haul. In far too many instances, beneficiaries end up going on spending sprees that can create fun memories but nothing of any lasting value.

Why Do People Do Estate Planning?

- So their money and assets are passed on to the people they love.

- To better provide for a spouse.

- To provide for children.

- To prevent family conflict.

- To protect their assets from predators.

- To plan for future health care benefits.

- To make their deaths less stressful on their families.

- To minimize the taxes their estates will pay.

Most People Haven't Done *Any* Estate Planning!

"I don't want to plan for my death," many people say to themselves, and indeed, they never plan for their deaths.

They engage in a trade-off. If they don't plan, they save themselves the work involved, but they will end up leaving their families with huge messes and problems that could have been avoided by proper planning. If they do plan, their families will enjoy the fruits of that effort to plan as well as the assets they receive.

Never let the thought of planning intimidate you and convince you to put it off. Find a qualified professional to help you. That's the first step. That can take time, but it will be the first step, and it will give you the motivation you might need to go through the process because you won't be alone in it if a qualified attorney is helping you. And you can get all your estate ducks in a row.

The numerous questions that can come to the mind of those thinking about drawing up a will can overwhelm them and cause them to put it off, but it's a different story when they have someone knowledgeable enough to guide them through the process. The questions will still be there, but your attorney will have the answers.

Get Your Estate Planning Ducks in a Row

So don't worry about the number of questions you have; concentrate on getting help answering them. And it's alright if you don't understand all the steps of the process; that's what your attorney will help you with. Don't be intimidated by all of it—just begin.

"I don't like legal documents," some may say, and I've heard that myself and can understand it; legal documents can be scary. But look at it this way: think of the documents not as great masses of unintelligible legalese but as your personal written plan, your road map, *your* rule book.

"I don't want to think about death," others say, and it's certainly not unusual for all of us to not relish thinking about death, especially our own. We all know, however, deep down, that not thinking about our future death doesn't make it go away. We all need to have the courage to realize our deaths are deadlines that will come, and they can come at any moment. I know from my experience with my clients that the key is taking the steps necessary to help spouses and children deal with that emotional event as smoothly as possible.

You are the head of your household. Your goal should be to make your death be the least stressful and confusing as you can possibly make it for your family.

"My family will figure it all out without me having to do any fancy planning," some may say. In reality, the planning doesn't have to be "fancy," but it should be complete enough to accomplish all your goals.

The key point I want to make here is that you have to plan when you *can*. If you wait until you're sick or incapacitated, your ability to do your planning may be quite diminished or become unnecessarily more difficult. Don't wait until you're in a hospital bed or struggling to remember the simplest things before you get serious about your planning.

Why Don't People Plan Ahead?

- They're focused on today.

- They think it's all about "death planning.

- They think their stuff will automatically go to whom they want it to go.

- They blindly hope any problmes will somehow take care of themselves when the time comes.

- They incorrectly think estate planning is for "rich" people only.

- They don't care because it will be someone else's problem

I'm Not Rich!
I Don't Have an "Estate!"

You may think this, but in reality, you have an estate, even if it's only your home. The word "rich" is a relative term, as I'm sure you'll agree. I learned that myself when I took my daughter to Kenya on a two-week mission trip. It became obvious very quickly that the poorest of us in the United States are rich compared to so many we encountered there.

Even if the home you own is not extravagant, it is still an important asset. You probably worked many years to pay it off, and it would be a shame to see it wasted in any way or lost to some unforeseen event.

Estate planning:
"You" planning as well as "them" planning

Your estate is not just your home or your personal belongings; it's about you as well. Estate planning isn't just about making sure your stuff gets to your loved ones no matter how little or much you have; it's about making sure you're taken care of too, and that means planning for your potential disability.'

None of us wants to be a burden to our loved ones, but we also don't want our assets needlessly wasted if we become disabled, and we certainly don't want the high costs of disability and nursing home care to deplete our estates to the point we can't help our loved ones.

You're Richer than You Think

Your estate consists of all that you own; take a minute to consider all of these and add them up.

- home
- automobiles
- jewelry
- antiques
- furniture
- cash
- CDs
- stock and bonds
- life insurance proceeds
- annuities
- IRAs
- 401(k)s
- second home
- rental property

You're richer than you think. Even if you're "poor" by your standards, you must plan so that your valuable assets—your mind and body—are taken care of in the event you can't care for yourself.

You truly do owe it to yourself to get your estate planning right, because there's more than just your assets at stake here. In addition to all your assets, your estate also consists of people, for example,

- yourself

- spouse

- children

- grandchildren

- close relatives

- nonrelatives you care deeply about

- charities you may want to leave something to

A proper estate plan doesn't simply dump all your assets into other people's laps when you die; you can "construct" it in such a way that it will take into account the circumstances of your assets and the people you have decided will receive them. So as you think about your planning, think about the different issues involved. You should carefully weigh:

- When should your loved ones get your assets?

- How much of them should they get?

- Should they get it all at once or over time?

- Will they ever be able to handle your bequests, or should it be given mostly to their children?

- Will my spouse know how to manage my assets when I die?

- Are my children responsible and mature enough to handle "large" sums of money or assets?

- Do they understand money management well enough to do so?

- Do I want any to be used specifically for my grandchildren?

- Do I want to build in incentives so my children get educations or save money for homes?

Where Do Most People Safeguard Their Estate Planning Documents?

- Their homes.

- Safe deposit boxes.

- Attorneys' offices.

I Don't Care What Happens to My Stuff (or Family) after I Die —I'm *Not* Planning

> "Adventure is just bad planning."
>
> —Ronald Amundsen (Antarctic explorer)

Very few will say, "I don't care what happens to my stuff after I die," but some actually think this. In blunt language, if you're thinking this, you're being very callous and uncaring toward your family.

No one can make anyone plan; we all have to want to plan. Experienced estate planning attorneys can help, but they can't force anyone to plan.

Those not interested in planning have to ask themselves if they want to leave behind legacies for their families that are stressful, emotional, messy, and expensive, or if they want to leave a legacy that is less stressful, less emotional, not messy, and less expensive.

It's in your hands; you are in control of how it goes for your family, either for bad or good.

Are you really sure you don't want to plan your legacy?

If I Die Without a Will, Where Will My Stuff Go?

If you are married with two children, your debts ar paid, and then:

- 1/3 goes to your spouse

- 1/3 goes to your first child

- 1/3 goes to your second child

This will leave your entire estate ungarded from your children's creditors, anyone they end up divorcing, their immaturity, their inexperience, and their bad money management practices.

Georgia Has an Estate Plan for You if You Don't Have One Yourself

> "Let our advance worrying become
> advance thinking and planning.
>
> —Winston Churchill

The laws regarding estate planning and wills go back centuries, but there are other rules that go back for centuries as well, and those are the rules that will apply to your estate if you die without a plan.

If you fail to do your own estate planning, the State of Georgia will supply one for you. When you die "intestate," without a will, your estate is subject to the laws of intestacy.

Problems with Georgia's Intestate Plan

Georgia's intestate plan raises several problems, the first of which is that your estate may not get to the people you wanted to receive it in the way and in the time you wanted. The second problem is that Georgia's plan doesn't protect your children's inheritances from:

- creditors

- bankruptcies
- divorces
- costs of your illnesses

In short, failing to plan doesn't mean you don't have a plan; you do have a plan, one forced on you by Georgia.

If you do your planning, you will be able to make the decisions about how your estate is handled and who will get it. Otherwise, Georgia's intestate plan will kick in, and its plan could easily put your estate in the wrong hands and at the wrong time.

The High Costs of Georgia's Free Plan

Georgia's intestate plan is free—at first. Its real costs will show up later in terms of the cost of cleaning up the mess it makes, and that will be far greater than what it would have cost you to do the planning the right way, your way, ahead of time.

Money isn't the only cost to this "free" plan. Consider,

- your family will have to spend dealing with the mess after you're dead;
- your beneficiaries could cause themselves and others heartaches by wasting your estate if they are too young, too inexperienced in handling money, or if they have no spending discipline;
- those to whom you wanted your estate to go to could end up with much less than you wanted;
- those to whom you didn't want to leave anything might end up benefitting much more than others.

It's Not about Legal Documents— It's about Protecting Your Family

Estate planning does involve a number of documents, but keep uppermost in your mind that these documents are not just long pages of legalese, they are about people and making sure your plans, desires, and goals are accomplished so your loved ones will benefit the most.

The documents are certainly vital in this matter; they must be done correctly, and they must also be well designed—customized to fit your specific situation and needs.

This is the reason you shouldn't think about the words on paper as much as you should think of the lives of your loved ones and how they will be favorably impacted and improved by what you leave behind. You will have control over who receives it, in what manner, and in the timing you decide on.

Make no mistake—your family will be improved by the high quality and care you put into your planning, or they will be damaged by its low quality or, even worse, its lack of existence.

Protecting Your Children's Inheritance from Creditors, Bankruptcy, Divorce, or Costs of Your Illnesses

> "When we are planning for posterity,
> we ought to remember the virture is not hereditary.
>
> —Thomas Paine

Actually, simply planning your estate is not sufficient; it must be done in the proper manner in order for it to do the most good.

This is the reason I stress that using generic, boilerplate, cookie-cutter documents will *not* result in the best outcome. In fact, their use could result in a situation not anywhere near what you would have ended up with if you had been guided through the estate planning process by an experienced attorney.

Most people don't have any idea of the numerous great things that can be accomplished by the full array of estate planning options, nor do they realize what dangers and problems can be avoided by good planning.

You want to leave your family better off after you die. Bad stuff—some predictable, some not—happens to people all the time, but proper estate planning can help you as well as your beneficiaries guard against that bad stuff.

You are older and wiser than your family. They look to you for wisdom and good decision making. Whether they want it or not, they need you to protect your estate for them. Many things can "attack" the estate you leave for your children and grandchildren. If you are forewarned of these dangers, you will be able to plan for them. When and if they come, you'll be able to rest easy that they will not destroy what you've worked so hard for over so many decades. You will know that your assets will do the maximum good for those you love.

This will happen, however, only if you plan ahead—and plan well.

History of Estate Planning

Planning for loved ones has been around for as long as mankind. When people began to accumulate wealth, they naturally became concerned about passing it on to their loved ones. Makes sense, doesn't it?

When people began to look into the future and wonder what would happened to their assets and their loved ones when they died, they started creating written documents to record what their desires, their "wills" were when it came to their property.

Before anyone can give anything away, he or she has to own it, so ownership rights have to be established. Some of the first established property rights were set down in the Old Testament, in Leviticus, Numbers, and Deuteronomy. This was a simple recognition that people have a right to what they want to do with their assets.

Wills and Estate Planning: As Old as History

One very early record of someone establishing how his assets would be dealt with when he dies is in Genesis 48, when Joseph and his sons, Manasseh and Ephriam, visited Joseph's father, Jacob.

Another old example of wills being discussed is in Hebrews 9:16–17 (ESV):

> For where a will is involved, the death of the one who made it must be established.

> For a will takes effect only at death, since it is not in force as long as the one who made it is alive.

The first verse describes the beginning of the probate process, and the second verse is a statement of when a will document actually has any authority over the deceased person's assets. These biblical statements are 100 percent accurate; they are exactly how wills are treated to this day. Amazing!

A stable society is the only place where wills will be relevant. If the society is constantly at war, in turmoil, or subject to famine, or if its members are living on just a subsistence level, it is highly unlikely anyone would accumulate assets beyond a few hand tools and other essentials. Even if someone did, an unstable society wouldn't be able to guarantee that someone's beneficiaries would receive those belongings; anyone more powerful could simply take them.

Thousands of years later, England played a prominent role in the evolution of wills and estates. No one is exactly sure how England's system of wills and estates and probate came into existence; The Roman Empire was the one truly major stable society that spanned from the apostle Paul's time to England. The Romans probably brought the legacy of wills that they found in ancient Israel, and then the Anglo-Saxons, who conquered the country later, certainly had an effect on the development of law in England.

The American colonies and later the United States generally modeled their system of wills after the one they received from England, so the legal principles underlying the system of wills and estates we have in the United States and more specifically in Georgia have remained largely consistent for centuries. When you pick up a will document, you are holding a modern document with deep historical roots.

Protecting from the Grave—How to Give Love and Wisdom after You're Gone

If you have grown children, you've experienced the progression of infants becoming toddlers, five-year-olds, teenagers, and finally adults.

Life changed as they grew. You don't deal with a twenty-five-year-old the same way you dealt with him or her as a teenager, a child, or an infant. We all hope that all our sons and daughters will grow into mature, responsible adults. We also know that while many do, some don't.

Our Hearts' Desires

We all want to help our children, not to harm them. The problem, however, is that when we die, they may receive more money and assets than they can handle, and that money could end up harming them. It's a fact that some may not be experienced enough to handle all the problems that can go wrong with life: creditor problems, divorces, bad economies, and other things they've never even thought of but that you know of firsthand or secondhand.

None of us wants to control our children or grandchildren from the grave, but we certainly want to protect them from making mistakes or suffering from the mistakes or maliciousness of others. Some mistakes take only moments to make but can have long-lasting effects; an automobile driving mishap could result in injuries to them or others; bad relationships, whether personal or business, could result in situations that can be difficult or impossible to recover from.

Guard Duty

Those who see the possibility of such problems must take the responsibility of planning for them on behalf of others. Someone going through the estate planning process can be likened to a lookout on a ship, scouring the seas for icebergs and other dangers to keep the ship safe.

You must ask yourself whether, as the head of your family, you have a similar duty to fulfill.

The Goals of Estate Planning

Even if our hearts are in the right place and we want to protect our families, we oftentimes don't know all the dangers we should be on guard for.

We should establish as our goal to achieve as many of our estate planning goals as we can. The process has a couple of steps, the first being to know what good goals are, and then to begin the process of seeking wise counsel so we can achieve as many of those goals as possible in the most efficient way possible by using the best tools for that particular job.

Let's get started.

Goal: No Surprises for Your Family

Dealing with the death of a loved one is difficult. Grieving over the loss is a sensitive time, and the last thing your family needs is unexpected surprises.

To reduce the chances of unpleasant surprises, proper, well-thought-out planning must be done ahead of time.

But that isn't enough, because even the best preplanning can catch your family unaware if they are unfamiliar with your financial affairs or have expectations about how your assets will be divided and whether or not those assets will be given in lump sums or otherwise.

You owe it to your family, and especially your spouse, to take time to bring them in to meet with you so you can explain where all the important papers are, and give them an idea of how your estate planning will distribute your assets.

This will allow them to mentally process, ahead of your death, what they will be finding out in more detail during their time of grief. This will help prevent them from perhaps being mentally and emotionally overloaded at that time.

Honesty Is the Best Policy

Such a meeting, perhaps one-on-one with each of your children, will allow you to "bring them down gently" if they will be receiving less than they may be thinking of your remaining assets. This may be the case if you are going to equalize your giving if in the past you have helped one child more than another. This will also be a good time to discuss if you are going to leave assets in trust for one child, when you might not be doing so for another child. This may be needed if the child is either irresponsible, in a bad marriage, or not good at managing money.

Some of these family conversations may be tense, but it is much better to have them now while you are here to directly speak with them, than to not have the conversation and the children not have any way to fully understand what your rationale was for your bequests.

This is not a time to "wimp" out. You must not let your fear of facing your family cause you to not hold these valuable family conversations and allow your estate planning bequests to surprise them later.

If dealt with correctly, this is a great time to discuss your values and what it is, besides mere assets, that you want your children to take away from your life.

Goal: Making Sure You Don't Accidentally Disinherit Your Children

Sometimes, the obvious solutions end up being the worst ones. Let's imagine you have money but you simply need help actually making sure your bills get paid. Your spouse has predeceased you, so you place one of your three children on your bank accounts as a co-owner so he or she can handle your banking.

Let's also imagine your will says your assets are to be divided equally among your three children. Sounds fine. But it won't happen.

When you die, the money in your bank accounts will not be controlled by your will; the child who is the co-owner will immediately own whatever is in your bank accounts.

That child *may* share this money equally with the others, but he or she doesn't have to and may not want to. Further no law requires it, and your will has no power over the situation.

All assets held in joint tenancy pass to the joint owner when the other owner dies by what is called an "operation of law"—it's automatic. Even if you didn't intend to, you will have in fact disinherited your children from a part of your estate, and it could be a big part.

While using joint tenancy and ownership may appear to be a quick or easy solution to some of life's issues or estate planning goals, the fact is that it can have just the reverse effect.

Goal: Not Accidentally Leaving Your Home to Just One Child

Some seniors place one of their sons or daughters on the deed to their homes. They think that if they place their most trusted child on the deed, that child will best take care of the home for the family after they die and will make sure it is divided equally among all the siblings. This is a mistake for several reasons.

If the son or daughter you place on your deed is helping you in other ways, he or she may, correctly or not, come to believe the house was payment for all the ways he or she has helped you and think you wanted him or her to have the home, not just a portion of it, after you die.

Another problem may be that despite their good intentions, after you die, one son or daughter may start thinking he or she deserves complete ownership of the house because you helped out this or that sibling of theirs at times in the past. One child may consider himself or herself to be the "responsible" one and thus deserving of an asset to even the score.

This "equalizing" scenario is not uncommon when one son or daughter has had addictions or life problems and has been given cash over the years. That cash added up, and the "responsible" child may view it as unfair to receive only one half of what's left after all that other cash had gone to the "irresponsible" child.

As a result, if a house, rental property, or a bank account is put into a son's or daughter's name, he or she may attempt to achieve "fairness" by deducting all the cash given to the other sibling before dividing the remainder between them.

This is one reason some estate planning attorneys strongly advocate that the parent "equalize" the estate by giving more to the responsible child since in fact the less-responsible child has already received a portion of the parents' estate through the extra help and cash given and received over the years.

Goal: Talking Frankly about Your Values with Your Children

Our goal should be to craft estate plans that let our loved ones know we care but that also help them understand and learn from us.

Each of us has certain values and beliefs about what's right and wrong, and we all have values that affect how we think our earthly resources should be used.

When you give your assets to your children or grandchildren, you will want them to know your views on how you want them to utilize what took you a lifetime to accumulate. Talking about intangibles such as values may seem a little touchy-feely, but it's nonetheless vitally important if you want to impart your values and beliefs to your descendants.

You have choices in regard to your values when it comes to estate planning: you can hope your loved ones use your resources in a manner you'd approve of, or you can structure your planning so your heirs will have no choice but to use the assets in a way acceptable to you.

We all want to protect and provide for our loves ones after we've died, and we also know that any planning we do that limits what they can do with the assets they receive is simply in their best interests. You aren't trying to limit them; you're trying to protect them.

Before the planning begins, ask yourself about your values are.

- What do you care about?
- What do you detest?
- What do you hold in high regard?
- What do you want your children to achieve?

These are just some of the questions you should think about when it comes to clarifying your desires for them. Once you have done that, you can pass on your values to the future generations of your family. You can tell them:

- you love them no matter what
- you care no matter what
- success isn't everything
- money isn't everything
- hard work is important
- sacrifice is essential
- delayed gratification is a sign of maturity
- some bad things can happen that are not their fault
- other bad things can happen that will be their fault, and they'll suffer the consequences

Anxiety and Discomfort

A *Wall Street Journal* article written by Anne Tergesen (June 11, 2012) dealt with the problem of families not discussing estate planning and inheritances.

> Not surprisingly, many families are loath to discuss these issues ... In addition to serving as a reminder of the older generation's mortality, a conversation about inheritance ... can provoke anxiety in parents. Many are uncomfortable disclosing the details of their finances.

> In turn, adult sons and daughters aren't eager to ask their parents about money for fear of coming across as greedy. Some feel guilty for thinking about their own financial needs at a time when parents could be facing steep medical or long-term-care expenses ...

> Nevertheless, financial advisers say, it is important for families to talk—if only to establish realistic expectations.

Yes, it's very important for families to talk and to establish expectations.

What Values Do You Want to Pass On to Your Children and Grandchildren?

- To learn to manage money?

- To enjoy delayed gratification?

- To avoid the "I just won the lottery!" mentality with inheritances?

- To live below their means?

- To not worry about keeping up with the Joneses (who are in debt anyway)?

- To think very hard about financial choices and decisions before they make them?

- To appreciate money and assets, which are hard to earn but easy to waste?

- To avoid spur-of-the-moment decisions, especially financial decisions?

- To pursue higher education (college or techinal)?

- To appreciate and support religious causes and quality charities?

Goal: Managing Joint Tenancy, Joint Accounts, and Other Types of Joint Ownership

Many people use joint tenancy or other forms of joint ownership without giving it any thought; they think of it simply as an easy solution to a problem. As I mentioned in the section "Goal: Making Sure You Don't Accidentally Disinherit Your Children," joint ownership means just that—joint ownership.

Some folks have a fantasy view of legal matters. They believe that if they place one of their children on their bank accounts or land that those children and everyone else will understand it was done only as a convenience for Momma or Grandma. That is 100 percent incorrect.

If they place anyone's name on an asset, that person gets ownership interest in it and can use it any way he or she sees fit.

On top of that, any creditor can seize it regardless of what either of the owners says.

There are significant dangers to placing assets and accounts in joint ownership situations I will go over with you here.

You'll No Longer Be in Control

The main consequence of placing an account, asset, or property in joint ownership with a child's or a grandchild's name is that you will no longer be in control of it.

Let's revisit the example I brought up earlier, of an elderly mother who needs help writing checks and reconciling bank statements and comes up with the seemingly easy solution of making one of her children co-owner of the account. This happens all the time; bank accounts, homes, land, rental homes, and business assets end up placed in joint ownership through this thinking.

However, making someone a joint owner of an asset opens the door to some very dangerous risks that neither the parent nor child has usually given any thought to.

Creditor Risks:
Your Stuff is No Longer Safe

Two events can impact such jointly held assets. One scenario is when the person added on to the account has financial problems he or she didn't mention to the parent out of embarrassment. That new co-owner could also think that the asset is safe "since it's really Mom's, not mine" or "I was only on the account to help Mom out."

Neither of these two rationales will help when a creditor sues the son or daughter and begins collection proceedings to seize the money (or the asset) shared with Mom.

Another scenario involves a son or daughter whose financial picture was good but who ends up with major financial problems due to unanticipated job losses, illnesses, business failures, divorces, and so on. Creditors can go after such assets.

I had a client whose grandmother placed the family land (which her house was sitting on) in the name of the grandson, but the grandmother didn't know the son hadn't filed income tax returns for years. She found out only after the IRS placed tax liens on her property. A creditor, in this case the IRS, will usually not settle a debt for less than it's owed if the debtor has full or partial ownership of a juicy asset or a big pool of money.

Creditors are unlikely to care that Junior was named as an owner of the asset just to help Mom out. They'll just swoop in like vultures, looking for anything they can grab, and they'll be happy when they find an account or asset Mom put Junior's name on. The creditor will seize it and fly away.

Even bankruptcy may be more of a danger than a solution. If a child, who is named as co-owner of an asset, ends up in financial difficulty and declares bankruptcy, the bankruptcy trustee will want to seize the account or asset and divide it among the creditors.

And by the way—bankruptcy trustees make nice fees for handling seizures, which is a strong motivation for trustees to look for any assets they can grab.

I've seen the IRS and the Georgia Department of Revenue grab joint accounts and assets. They love that Mom had been so unwittingly generous and that a back tax liability can be paid off.

Divorce

People are never any meaner, less merciful, or less reasonable than during a divorce; such an emotionally charged situation seems to bring out the devil in many.

Both parties to divorce proceedings often believe they have been terribly wronged, and they want retribution for their injuries. For this reason, they'll go after any asset they can find even if they know it doesn't really belong to their soon-to-be ex, for example, bank accounts that person shares with a parent or land that is held jointly.

Divorces often get real messy real fast. The lawyers will make lots of money attempting to defend Mom's bank accounts, and your lawyers may or may not be successful. It mostly depends on how the judge feels that particular day and how much the judge dislikes Mom's child on one side of the courtroom or the "injured" spouse on the other.

You never want to be in a situation in which other parties are clawing after your assets that you put in someone else's name so that person could help you, not hurt you. But those seeking those assets for whatever reason will not care.

I Never Thought My Child Would Do That!

Sometimes, we think we know others, especially our children, very well, but people can and they certainly do change. Even the nicest people sometimes fall into addictions. Drugs and alcohol can be a problem a child can try to hide, but it's still there, waiting to burst out.

Gambling as well has become a widespread scourge; it's become more accepted and "main streeted" through lotteries, casinos, and online poker games.

I've had numerous clients whose spouse or child racked up large debt on the clients' credit cards and emptied out bank accounts. Children sometimes "borrow" money from joint accounts they may have the best of intentions of repaying, but they rarely ever gain or regain the ability to do so.

This can be a big financial threat; large sums of your money can vanish in the blink of an eye. I met a man whose accounts had been cleaned out between one bank statement and the next; the client found out after the fact that the money was spent at an out-of-state casino. The only way he'd have been able to catch the theft would have been by checking his balance every day, and no one wants to live like that. However, people can be vulnerable to that kind of theft in co-ownership situations, or even when only signature authority has been given to another person.

Just as a child might have no financial problems today but could have them tomorrow, a child with no drug or gambling problem could develop one next week, month, or year.

Can't Finance or Refinance, or Sell the Property

An unforeseen consequence of having someone on the deed for your home or other real estate is that you won't be able to finance or refinance the asset with a lending institution without the permission of the other person. That's because the lending institution will require both owners to sign, and your other owner might not want to have a loan taken out on it! You could end up being held hostage by the person you made co-owner.

You won't be able to sell the property either unless your co-owner gives consent, and that person might not want to sell what is now his or her property.

When these types of events occur, they are quite shocking to the mother or whoever put the other person on the deed; the original owner may have thought he or she was in control of the asset but ends up not due to the joint title.

Some Heirs May Get More, and Some May Be Disinherited

Due to joint tenancy, some of your heirs may get a larger share of your assets than you intended, and some may end up accidentally disinherited. I discuss this in depth in the section that deals with accidentally or partially disinheriting an heir.

Joint Ownership—Bad for Medicaid Planning

You should also be aware that placing accounts or assets in joint tenancy ownership may cause planning problems if you need to qualify for Medicaid.

Avoid Joint Tenancy—Good Alternatives Exist

The simple fact is that there are much better ways than joint tenancy that will accomplish your needs and not leave you vulnerable and in a position of having to pay for others' mistakes, bad judgment, and financial difficulties. An experienced estate planning attorney can guide you through different options and help you decide which is best for your specific situation.

Goal: Avoiding Family Conflicts

When life is easy, everything seems peaceful, but when challenging events occur in a family, they can often bring about tensions, misunderstandings, high emotions, hurt feelings, and outright conflicts that affect them all.

Disagreements about Your Care if You Are Disabled

An example of one of these challenging events is when your health declines. Very commonly, others think they know exactly what you'd want done in a particular circumstance. Your family may love you deeply, they may even love each other deeply, but they also may deeply care that the "right" thing gets done for you. The problem is that they can disagree as to what that "right" thing is.

This is where good planning can come to the rescue. If you have planned for medical situations like this carefully, there should never be a circumstance in which your family members are wondering what the "right" thing to do is—you will have already clearly laid it all out for them.

Your family members faced with your stressful life events will find it very comforting to know exactly what your wishes were in every circumstance. It's easy to see that this lifts the responsibility off their shoulders and makes the risk of disagreement almost nonexistent.

Disagreements about Your Funeral Arrangements

The same can be said for something as "simple" as handling your funeral arrangements. How can your family members know what you wanted unless you have memorialized it in your planning documents?

This as well takes a tremendous burden off those you will leave behind. A tremendously sorrowful and stressful time in your loved ones' lives can be made much less stressful by your careful planning.

What's a "Fair" Inheritance? Heirs Can Disagree

After you have died, your loved ones may formulate opinions about how fairly you have treated them based on what you have left them.

You may have left them equal shares, but if you assisted one or the other over the years and that's not reflected in your will, that could cause discontent. The others may think that particular sibling ended up receiving more than they did, and in pure dollar amounts, they may be correct. But they may think that they have been "punished" because they didn't need any monetary assistance from you when you were alive.

This same scenario can happen when one son or daughter received financial assistance from you to go to college but another didn't. Your children who didn't receive college money from you may think they ended up receiving less than those who did.

Whether these feelings are correct or not is for you to decide, but I caution you not to ignore such feelings; they can cause hard feelings among your beneficiaries after you're gone, and that's not the memory you want them to associate with you and your decisions.

It's straightforward enough, although not easy, to avoid this problem by speaking to your children at an appropriate time in their lives about what they can expect to receive and why they will receive a certain amount or percentage.

All that said, you should strongly consider "equalizing" the inheritances if you are able.

Goal: Making Sure Your Inheritances Aren't Squandered

Time to Party?

Parents work hard all their lives to provide decent lives for themselves and their children. Many parents want to leave inheritances to their children to help them get head starts in life; they want to give them the assistance they might need to build successful lives and better themselves. They hope their children will use inherited money to increase their education, buy a home, pay off a mortgage, save for their own retirement, and other noble goals.

Research, however, has shown that this is most often not what happens. Most of the time, inherited money doesn't last long at all; it's usually squandered on things that wouldn't be considered priorities in the eyes of the parents who had earned that money and had passed it on.

Confessions of Inheritance Wasters

Lost inheritances are very sad; they represent what could have been if the money had been put to smarter uses. They represent missed opportunities. They represent lifetimes of assets gathered by one person but frittered away in extremely short times by others.

Some sad articles detailing confessions of how young, inexperienced, or careless people wasted their inheritances can be found online.

"I Spend my $66,000 Inheritance on Basically Nothing" Allison Cinting, May 4, 2012

thebillfold.com/2012/05/i-spent-my-66000-inheritance-on-basically-nothing/

"How I Blew Through $100,000 Before I Turned 21" Jacob Wade, June 12, 2012

www.iheartbudgets.net/2012/06/how-i-blew-through-100000-before-i-turned-21/

"Man Regrets Wasting $100,000 Inheritance at the Mall" AOL Business

on.aol.com/video/man-regrets-wasting--100-000-inheritance-at-the-mall-517799204

He says he spent $1,000 per month just at the food court.

"I blew my Million-dollar Inheritance" Alex Lasarev, the *Guardian*, June 18, 2010

hwww.theguardian.com/lifeandstyle/2010/jun/19/blew-million-dollar-inheritance

"I inherited a Fortune and then Frittered it all Away" Katie Sampson, the *Guardian*, September 27, 1994

www.independent.co.uk/life-style/i-inherited-a-fortune-
and-then-frittered-it-all-away-1439995.html

Lost Inheritances—So Many Horror Stories

I recommend that you read the Trust Advisor online newsletter
"Lost Inheritances—Studies Show Americans Blow Through
Family Fortunes at a Remarkable Rate" at thetrustadvisor.com/
tag/inheritance

The article says that in an attempt to find an answer to why heirs
oftentimes quickly waste their inheritances, researchers at the
Williams Group, a family-wealth consultancy, did a survey of more
than 2,000 families over a twenty-year period. It found that high
taxes and poor investment advice were not the biggest factors;
it found that 60 percent of the time, trust and communication
breakdown issues among family members played the biggest
roles.

> It's not hard to imagine squabbling siblings, mired in
> childhood resentments and rivalries, who can't agree …

> They sometimes end up not speaking to each other at
> all. "Wealth is a magnifier … If you have problems, it will
> magnify them."

The same study reports that 25 percent of the time, the banana
peel turned out to be the families' failure to prepare heirs for their
pending prosperity.

According to a 2012 study by U.S. Trust, more than half had not
fully disclosed their wealth to their offspring, while another 13
percent kept completely mum about it.

The article says parents aren't talking with their children about their assets and estate, which is understandable, some say, since many parents fear that if they spill the beans to their kids too soon, they risk creating a brood of spoiled layabouts.

But Jim Grubman, a veteran family-wealth counselor based in Turner Falls, Massachusetts, says such discretion often backfires. In his experience, no timeframe for disclosure works unless the children have been given some ongoing messages about money and how to deal with it. An unprepared inheritor's reaction to the news, he says, can range from a deer-in-the-headlights paralysis to uncontrolled spending benders—not to mention addiction and depression. "There are so many horror stories," he says.

The hard fact is that you'll never know how your children will spend their inheritance if you give it to them in a lump sum no matter how well you've raised them to handle money. You can keep them from trouble and give them an opportunity to learn some responsibility by giving them their inheritances in a wiser fashion.

Goal: Getting a Handle on the Different Estate Planning Documents

Clients often have a hard time understanding their estate planning documents though we try our best to ensure they do. They can be complex, but that's because they aren't just piles of paper written by attorneys; they are special legal documents that carry with them the force of law; they are legally enforceable.

Each document is designed to accomplish a specific purpose. The reason you should take the time to ask questions and learn about your planning documents is because that will help you take advantage of the unique help each one can provide you and your estate when the proper time has arrived for it to become activated or used.

Think about your estate planning documents as tools that can help you accomplish certain tasks, and you need to know what each one of them can accomplish. Most important, you want only high-quality tools that were specifically designed to handle your particular situation and needs.

A common problem is that people think they have all such estate tools they need, but they end up sadly mistaken. It is only later, when those tools are actually needed, that they or their family discover the tools were poorly made or assembled, or too generic, or not really designed for their special planning needs.

Goal: Understanding the Changing Definitions of "Family"

In these changing times, it's no longer sufficient to slap together an estate planning document without putting the necessary thought into the process. Doing that simply means someone has left out the "planning" part of "estate planning." That's a recipe for disaster; it's very likely that you won't accomplish what you wanted, and your family may be left with a real mess on its hands that results in heartache for those you love.

Life Isn't Simple Anymore

When it comes to estate planning, blindly using generic phrases or generic documents won't accomplish what you want them to. Just as life has changed, so has estate planning. This is the age of blended families; what that means is that the statement "This is my son" may not mean that at all. It may mean stepson, adopted son, foster son, illegitimate son, or something else.

Experienced estate planners don't forget that divorces and nonmarital relationships may have occurred, and that when you use the word "children," you may mean just your own blood children, not a stepson or a foster daughter.

One way the world has changed over the decades is reflected in the divorce rate. A high divorce rate coupled with the remarriages of divorced people has resulted in what we now call the blended family, one in which at least one spouse has children from a different marriage or cohabitation. These families have different dynamics than do families that have not suffered divorces.

The estate planning for a blended family must be carefully crafted and reviewed to avoid unintended results. This is true not only for the spouses of blended families but also for the grandparents thinking about leaving assets to their children who are the spouses in a blended family.

Most grandparents strongly want their assets to stay in their bloodline or with their blood heirs. Special planning must be crafted to ensure that this goal is accomplished even after the grandparents have died.

Accidental Disinheriting of Children

Another drawback of using generic, "off the shelf," noncustomized forms in estate planning is assets being left to a surviving spouse who may unintentionally disinherit the children who are not biologically his or hers. There may be no animosity involved; it could be due to poor financial planning on the part of the surviving spouse, but creditors will grab any and all they can, and the result could be that children's inheritances are lost.

It's for such reasons (and many more, actually) that you must be thorough and careful with your estate planning process, not lazy and haphazard. An experienced estate planner can be of great assistance in helping you craft a plan for your estate that will survive challenges.

Goal: Striking Equality with Your Benefactors' Inheritances

What does "equal" mean?

Most of the time, clients want to divide their estates among their children equally. But a problem is that "equally" may not be a good idea. Why? Let's look at some scenarios.

Scenario 1: College

I mention elsewhere how paying for college for one child can cause resentment in another child who didn't receive college funding from you. In truth, if you divide the estate equally, you are indeed shortchanging the child who didn't receive the benefit of having tuition, books, and room and board paid for four years. That's a chunk of money that child didn't get; equal inheritances don't take this into consideration.

Scenario 2: Punishing success

Say, for instance, one child had a drug or drinking problem, and you helped that child out plenty over the years by paying for alcohol or drug rehabilitation or with cash when he or she was unemployed or underemployed.

You may have forked over money to pay fines and lawyers for that child, perhaps a great deal over the years, so maybe another child shouldn't be penalized by receiving an equal share that doesn't take into account the extra expenses the other child had created.

Scenario 3: Inheritances from in-laws or grandparents

A situation sometimes arises that the spouse of one of your children receives an inheritance from his or her parents. If it's large enough, you should perhaps consider whether this should affect how much you leave to that child; you might consider leaving more to your other children.

The same scenario can happen with grandchildren who receive inheritances from their grandparents on the other side of the family. This could prompt you to consider giving a larger portion to other grandchildren to compensate for this.

Scenario 4: Loans never repaid

Another scenario is when a child (or grandchild) is lent money that never gets repaid. This child will in essence could receive more from you if you divide what you give to your children without taking this unpaid debt into consideration.

Solutions

All these situations, and many others that revolve around this concept of "equality" can be resolved. You can calculate as best you can how much you've helped your sons and daughters out over the years individually and take those amounts into consideration when you're calculating how much you will be leaving each. Maybe one child gets 60 percent and another gets 40 percent instead of equal shares; perhaps one gets 40 percent and two others get 30 percent each to reflect your contributions to their welfare over the years.

No matter what, you shouldn't for a second think your children won't care. They may say they don't care, but they will. Their feelings may be hurt, or they may bear a grudge, maybe small, maybe large, against their siblings, and that's not a result you want.

Lacking Cash to Make Things Even

In the event your estate might not have the cash to "even" things up with your beneficiaries, consider writing up your estate plan in such a way that the proceeds from a life insurance policy can be used to even things up, but this, again, requires good planning and good advice.

In the end, treating your children equally doesn't necessarily mean leaving them equal amounts. You do have a responsibility to truly treat them equally, but that could mean not giving them equal amounts at your death.

Your children are different; they will have differing needs over their years as kids, teenagers, young adults, and parents, and that means you should at least consider whether giving them equal shares is the proper thing. It very well may be, but it might not be.

Should Your Childrent Get Equal Shares of Your Estate?

Matters to Consider:

- Did you put one but not another through college?

- Will you be punishing the success of one?

- Did you already grant some inheritance in the form of a loan that wasn't paid back?

- Did you spend money helping one overcome an addiction to gambling, drugs or with legal problems?

- Has one already received and inheritance from a parent or a grandparent on the other side of the family?

Goal: Making Sure a Grandchild's Bequest Is Not Wasted by a Child

Grandparents often want to help their grandchildren as well as their children, but when they make their children "trustees" for what they want to leave to their grandchildren, problems can arise. Someone who does that could be placing too much trust in their children, and as a result, there may be nothing left for their grandchildren.

There are a number of ways your sons or daughters might spend what you've intended your grandchildren to receive. Consider these scenarios:

Scenario 1: "That's not an extravagance!"

Most people aren't as careful with their money as you are. Your children may think that purchasing a vacation home or taking a long family vacation on a cruise ship makes perfect sense, whereas you could see that as an extravagant expenditure in light of their financial situation.

Seniors usually think that an upscale car or extra-nice house may be a luxury, but some people view things like that as simply enjoying the nicer things of life.

If, however, the beneficiaries of your estate repeat this same financial behavior and purchasing pattern time after time over five, ten, twenty years, they will spend that money faster than you could imagine.

Scenario 2:
A budget? What's that?

Your children may not be as budget-minded as you are. They may not know how to live within their means. They may view their inheritances as big pots of money to "borrow" from. They might have great intentions of repaying that "bank," but their lack of money management skills might prevent them from ever being able to do that.

The children may mean well, but over time, the drip, drip, drip of money leaking out will cause even the biggest pot of money to run dry, and as a result, they have little or nothing to leave to their children, your grandchildren.

Scenario 3:
Children's bankruptcy

Even if children mean well, know how to manage money, and can live on a budget, so many unexpected events can come up out of nowhere. Catastrophic health care expenses or other unplanned disasters can lead to lawsuits or bankruptcy, and your inheritance money might get sucked up by creditors or the bankruptcy court since the money you had wanted to leave to your grandchildren is in your children's names.

Scenario 4:
Children's divorce

Unfortunately, people fall out of love all the time. Spouses make foolish decisions and commit adultery. People you've known for decades suddenly act differently or make decisions they would seemingly never have made in the past. This, we all know, is life, and it can lead to divorce. The next bad news is that your son's or daughter's inheritance money has become part of the family pot of money being argued over.

The Same Result

All these different scenarios result in the same thing—your grandchildren getting nothing. But it didn't have to end like that. Good planning could have easily prevented all these disasters; it could have prevented what you wanted to leave to your grandchildren from being spent unnecessarily or seized by creditors or ex-spouses.

Goal: Avoiding Problems Caused by Leaving Real Estate Jointly to Children

When estate planners ask most parents what they want to do with their homes when they die, most of those parents will say they want to leave them to their children equally. However, leaving a house in equal shares to children can bring about a set of problems.

The first is that your children might not want to keep your home because they:

- couldn't live there—too many memories of you

- need the cash from the sale of the house

- don't like the location of the house

- don't like its floor plan

- think the house looks old or dated

- think the house is too small or too large

- think the house is too far away from work

- already have a house they like

And even in the case in which one of your children wants the house, that child might not qualify for financing to "buy out" the siblings, and the siblings might not want to owner-finance the house. This can create bad blood among the children, which is the last thing you wanted to "give" them.

An alternative strategy that also often doesn't work out is when the children decide to rent the house out. Conflicts can arise when one child thinks the others aren't doing their part to manage the home which has become a business, a rental house. One child may end up doing uncompensated work on the house, or the majority of work when dealing with renters, such as cleaning the house between renters, doing repairs, or dealing with contractors to handle the repairs. This may be due to the fact that some siblings live out of the state where the property is located, but it's still a recipe for bad feelings.

You may own a rental house or a commercial building you lease out, and the same situation can apply to this type of real estate. Your first inclination may be to leave this asset to your children in equal shares, but you have to consider the circumstances when weighing this option versus selling the asset and splitting up the cash or other options.

Some of your children might need immediate cash, not just a share of the rent the property generates, so their first choice might be to sell the asset. However, other siblings might prefer to hold onto the asset as investment property. If so, they will be, in essence, holding their siblings' desires hostage; this can seem unfair to those who want the asset sold. If none of the siblings has the cash or credit to buy out the siblings who want out of owning the property, they could be forced into a property ownership situation that they want no part of, and this could create ongoing hard feelings.

As is the case with the family house, perhaps a fairer plan would be to arrange for the sale of the property at your death and the splitting up of the proceeds. Any of your children who want to take their share of the cash from the sale and invest in rental or investment property will be free to do so, while those who prefer cash will get that too.

If the children decide to keep the property, they need to discuss important matters that will result from that decision. Will one heir manage the property? Will that heir be paid? If so, how much? What will be expected of the manager? How will the other siblings know they're getting their money's worth of those services?

You won't be around to help them in such a situation, so consider spending good time in discussion with them on these matters and give them the benefit of your counsel.

If they cannot agree on how the above items will be worked out, or if disagreements arise, you can advise them to hire a professional property management firm. This option may be the difference between future happy or tense Thanksgivings in the future.

The rule of thumb here is that it's generally not good to tie heirs together with a joint ownership asset, and that goes for rental property, investment property, and vacation homes in addition to your home.

Frequently, the best course of action is to have your estate plan call for the trustee or executor to sell the house or property and divide the proceeds among your children. This will allow each to do as he or she pleases with the cash, and it will remove any chance that conflict will arise because of this issue.

Goal: Equalizing Bequests When Leaving Assets with Differing Levels of Debt

Parents often want to leave their assets in equal monetary shares to each sibling; to do so, they have to value each asset. If an asset has debt attached to it, they need to come up with a net value for that asset.

Let's say an estate includes two pieces of real estate both valued at $100,000 but one has a mortgage of $30,000 and the other has a mortgage of $80,000. One has a net value of $70,000, while the other weighs in at $20,000. This value difference must be taken into consideration when you decide to will them to children.

Some estates will include enough cash to pay down the debt on one property to match the debt on the other, or if your estate lacks sufficient cash to do this, you can plan ahead and take out a life insurance policy aimed at achieving exactly that.

The fact is that there are ways to handle situations in which assets are unequal, say, due to mortgages or debt, and an experienced estate planner well experienced in the law and knowledgeable about the facts of your situation can be of tremendous help.

Equal Value, but Unequal Growth Potential

Even if both properties are valued at the same amount, and each has the same debt or is free of debt, the two properties may still be unequal due to the different potentials they have to appreciate. If one asset is growing in value while the other is stagnant or declining in value, they soon will become unequal in value, and you have to take this into consideration when you plan on giving one to one child and the other to another. (This, by the way, is a good reason to review your will periodically so you can take such changes in value into consideration and change your will accordingly.)

This is another case in which the proceeds from a life insurance policy could be used to remedy this issue after your death, or one or both assets could be sold so your children receive the same amount of cash and invest it as they see fit.

If you believe you are more savvy when it comes to real estate than your children, you may want to sell such real estate (or other assets) since you will be in a better position to strike good deals.

Don't forget that most people prefer cash to hard assets. This doesn't mean that a child who prefers cash is a bad money or asset manager; it's simply a recognition that some folks don't want to deal with hard assets. If the asset is sold, the cash can go toward stocks, bonds, or mutual funds that can appreciate while offering a greater degree of liquidity than real estate does.

I don't have an opinion either way, but you should take the time to consider all sides of this issue and make a decision that you are comfortable with

Goal: Keeping Children from Wasting Inheritances

The ability to manage money doesn't necessarily increase as a person ages. Some people, no matter their age, never learn to manage money. This fact can be described as a simple equation:

Money + Immaturity = Disaster.

Here's how it often plays out:

- You pass away.
- Your heir receives a lump-sum inheritance.
- It's in a bank account.
- Now it's not in that bank account.
- It's gone. Wasted.

Scenario 1:
Certain children won't work or they waste money

Or perhaps they can't hold a job. But to make matters worse, they have never learned the value of a dollar. They've sponged off you for years, much to the frustration of their siblings, who feel these others have been financially babied way too much.

They never seem able to stand on their own two feet; they can't save a dollar because they're always seeing stuff they absolutely "need."

If such heirs were given outright inheritances—no matter their age—they'd burn through it in short order. Such heirs need protection—from themselves.

Scenario 2:
Some sons or daughters work hard but just can't save a dime

They work hard but spend just as hard for all kinds of reasons. They appear to be doing so many other things right, but their bad spending habits severely hinder their ability to save for the more practical things in life. While they may be hard working and pulling down good salaries, they're living paycheck to paycheck. They too need built-in barriers to protect their inheritances from being wasted.

Scenario 3:
A child has a drug or alcohol problem

Some sons or daughters have drug or alcohol or gambling problems that can be quite scary; they are just not capable of living productive lives much less handling outright inheritances. Such dependency problems must be taken into consideration when it comes to estate planning; otherwise, inheritances could be absolutely squandered. Worse than that, the money could simply make it easier for him or her to get into even greater danger due to a sudden influx of cash (or other assets) that would go to support their harmful habits.

Goal: Having Quality Power of Attorney Documents

The estate planning you do should address all the stages of your remaining life, including the possibility of physical and mental disability as well as the inevitability of your death.

If you should become mentally incapacitated, you will need someone with the legal authority to make financial decisions on your behalf.

While a stock, boilerplate, or bare-bones financial power of attorney may give your agent some of the needed authority to protect your interests, it is a poor substitute for a properly drafted, customized document that takes into account all circumstances—those you can foresee and also those you cannot foresee.

If you become mentally incapacitated before drafting a properly customized financial power of attorney, your agent will be completely unable to perform some duties to protect your estate.

Limited vs. Nonlimited Power of Attorney

An important example of the importance of a proper power of attorney comes up with Medicaid planning. A standard financial power of attorney will not give your agent enough power and authority because it is attempting to safeguard you from their "self-dealing," that is, your agent performing actions that end up being self-serving for him or her and detrimental to you. They could even get the authority to gift assets to themselves. As long as you trust the person who is acting as your agent, presumably a trusted child, there is no danger in giving your agent these much-more broader powers. These are exactly the actions you would have to take anyway to safeguard your assets.

Careful Evaluation Required

You have to evaluate your situation carefully to be able to determine how much you can trust the person you are considering selecting as your financial agent. You can give them limited authority, make the grant of authority much broader, or customize each component of it.

No matter which course of action you followed in creating the document, you should discussed the matter at length with an experienced estate planner who is also well versed in elder law and Medicaid planning so all bases are covered.

The decision to grant a limited authority versus an almost unlimited authority in your financial power of attorney is very important not only for you but also for your agent.

No matter which type of financial power of authority you give, you should include specific instructions to your agent so the agent won't be operating in the dark. Your agent in turn will have greater confidence when acting on your behalf with a set of instructions that lay out some of the principles you want followed.

These instructions will also serve as a way to hold your agent accountable when it comes to performing duties as you expect; your agent's actions can also be evaluated on the basis of your instructions by your heirs.

Things to Consider When Selecting a Financial Agent

- Is the person honest, even when no one is watching?

- Does the person share your views on how money should be managed? Will he or she go along with your philosophy of how to deal with money?

- Does the person have money problems?

- Is the person stable careerwise?

- Does the person have experience handling the amount of money and assets you need managed?

- Does the agent have a criminal background?

- Does the agent have any kind of financial conflict of interest with you?

Goal: Making Sure Your Children Receive Their Inheritances if Your Spouse Remarries

Many people like being married; it's absolutely true that we all yearn to be loved and to have companionship with someone we consider a best friend. For this reason, surviving spouses frequently consider remarrying if and when they find someone special.

While remarriage after the death of a spouse is, on the face of it, a personal issue between your spouse and his or her future spouse, the event may drastically affect your children and grandchildren if it affects your estate plans.

One of the most common concerns I hear clients ask is, "Is there a way to make sure my spouse doesn't accidentally lose part of our estate to a new spouse (and disinherit our children) if he (or she) remarries?"

There are several possible ways to make sure this potential problem never comes up. With proper planning, your spouse can still enjoy companionship after you pass away but protect the family money and ensure that it is used to support your spouse and leave a legacy for your children.

This is, of course, another reason that careful estate planning done by an experienced attorney is necessary, but once you have crafted your will or trust under such expert guidance, you'll have peace of mind on the issue.

Goal: Making Sure Children Don't Receive Inheritances at Too Young an Age

An inheritance gained hastily in the beginning will not
be blessed in the end.

—Proverbs 20:21 ESV

And the younger of them said to his father, "Father,
give me the share of property that is coming to me."
And he divided his property between them.

—Luke 15:12 ESV

The fact is that many basic, "off the shelf" estate plans don't properly deal with how to leave assets, money, or insurance proceeds to minors. Inheritances must be passed on prudently or they could be wasted by a young heir who could be taken advantage of. Young people may be able to vote at age eighteen, but that doesn't mean they know how to manage large inheritances; that ability comes with age and experience.

Ask yourself, "Is my child financially savvy enough to handle a large, lump sum if I died today?" I can tell you stories about inheritances that took a lifetime to acquire but only a few short years to lose. Most clients have as their goal to help their children attain the best chance of success in life while simultaneously safeguarding their assets so they can do the most good for their children for the longest period of time.

Careful thought must go into planning for minor or young heirs. Setting up proper trusts can be an invaluable tool used to achieve this goal.

I'm recommending here that you think outside the box on this matter, because rarely is a young person able to handle a lump sum of money, large or not. Consider some of the options available to you. You can distribute an inheritance:

- in certain sums over many years

- at certain stages of life, i.e., graduation from college or technical school, or after holding a job for a minimum period of years

- upon reaching certain ages, i.e., twenty-five, thirty-five, and so on.

- a little at a time, and just when needed as judged by and under the guidance of a trustee

- many other options

Goal: Making Sure Life Insurance Proceeds Are Handled Properly

I strongly support your using life insurance as a tool to help provide for your family when you die. After you buy the policy, you should periodically verify that the proper persons are designated as the beneficiaries of the policy's proceeds. This is because that as life goes on, children are born, divorces take place, and event occur that may alter your decision about beneficiaries of your life insurance.

If you decide that the beneficiaries of your insurance proceeds are minors or people unable to handle large sums of money, you should plan for this or realize that after you die, it's highly likely that the money will be lost through mismanagement.

You should consider creating a trust to hold the funds so they will be given out at proper times but not in a large lump sum that could be wasted or stolen by "friends" who want to help. A trust will allow you to exercise control over the money, whether it's a large amount or a modest amount, even after you are gone.

Goal: Not Giving Too Much, Too Soon to Children

A wonderful tool for clients is to set up what I call "incentive" trusts that encourage their children and grandchildren to attend college or a tech school. If the children and grandchildren are ambitious enough to attend college or get technical training, there will be money to pay for this specifically.

Sometimes it is wise to decide to leave money to beneficiaries in stages, that is, a certain amount goes to them every three or five years. The thinking behind this is that even if a younger person blows through the first installment that was left for him or her, perhaps five years later, that person will be wiser and a better money manager.

There are a number of reasons you might want to "spread out" what you want to leave to someone, and there are a number of creative ways of doing so to avoid the "too much too soon" inheritance that could harm your loved ones.

Goal: Naming Guardians for Minor Children

Estate planning isn't just for seniors; anyone with minor children must plan as well. To continually put off making such plans puts you at the risk of having a court get involved in deciding with whom your children will be placed should you die prematurely.

Grandparents in particular should consider this issue to be so important that they should consider actually taking their children who have minor children (your grandchildren) to an experienced estate planning attorney and paying for the planning. Consider this money well spend and good "insurance" for your grandchildren.

Careful consideration should be given to the selection of those you choose to serve as "substitute parents" for your children. You should ask yourself, "Who will be best able to raise my children in a manner I approve of?"

Those you select to be substitute parents for your children must be very responsible. The mere fact that you like them doesn't mean they should be selected because so much is at stake here. These folks will take care of not only your children's physical wellbeing, but their mental and spiritual wellbeing as well. You will want them to have the same moral values as you do and be willing and able to impart them to your children.

It would be great if those you choose as your children's guardians know how to manage money as well. They may be in charge of any government benefits your children are receiving or will receive in addition to what you leave for them. They may be tasked with handling your life insurance proceeds, but I would strongly suggest that you put these funds in a trust.

I've listed other consideration in the breakout boxes relating to guardians.

Guardians

- Are we responsible for caring for and raising your children

- will impart their valies, which should be yours, to your children

- may be in charge of any goverment benefits your children are receiving or will receive

- may be in charge of your life insurance proceeds (unless they are put into a trust)

What to Consider When Selecting Someone as Guardian

- What are this person's values?

- Religious beliefs?

- Background?

- Do your children know this person?

- How stable is this person (i.e. divorces, job history)?

- Can he or she manage money?

- How well do you really know this person?

- Have you talked with this person about guarduanship? Is he or she willing to be a guardian?

- Will your children relocate to the guardian's home?

- What is the potential guardian's parenting style?

Goal: Understanding Adult Guardianship and Conservatorship

Good News and Bad News

The good news is we're living longer. The bad news is we're living longer. We all run the risk that our bodies will outlast our brains.

We modern Americans are blessed in that we will live longer than any generation before; medical science has made it possible for our physical bodies to live for years longer than was thought possible just decades ago.

The downside is that while modern science has developed many marvelous ways to keep our bodies alive, our brains will oftentimes fail before our bodies do.

Mental but Not Physical Disability

This can lead to a circumstance in which your body may be physically able to carry out your daily activities but your brain is no longer able to function sufficiently to control your body.

This might develop into a situation in which someone becomes mentally incompetent but does not need a nursing home. This person may be ambulatory, able to "get around" well, but may have a greatly diminished mental capacity. The possibility of a brain failing before a body does is a very likely scenario today.

For those no longer able to make decisions for themselves despite being physically able-bodied, adult guardianship and adult conservatorship proceedings will have to be initiated so someone can make decisions on their behalf.

Living Probate

The process of filing for a guardianship or conservatorship is commonly called "living probate," because both of these processes must be initiated with the probate court that has jurisdiction over both these matters.

To differentiate between living probate and the probate process that occurs only after your death (your beneficiaries will submit your will to the probate court), the latter process is sometimes call "death" probate.

Legal Intervention

The hard truth is that you will have failed to plan if your loves ones have to appeal to a court for legal guardianship. It means that by your inaction, you forced your family to resort to legal intervention simply because there was no proper preplanning documents created they could use instead of going to court. This scenario can be avoided by careful planning.

Court action will be the only solution when you are unable to make decisions for yourself and no one has authority to act on your behalf. The probate court proceeding is easy to avoid *if* you take action.

Adult Guardianship and Adult Conservatorship

If you are no longer able to take care of your daily affairs because you are not of sound mind, someone may file a petition with the probate court to be appointed as guardian or conservator.

If the court approves the petition, you will be called the "ward." The court will grant your guardianship if it determines you lack sufficient mental capacity to make or communicate significant responsible decisions concerning your health or safety.

Likewise, the court may grant someone to be your conservator if it finds you lack sufficient capacity to make or communicate responsible decisions for the management of your money, income, or property.

Adult guardianship involves control over a person, while adult conservatorship involves control over the person's money.

Your guardian will have a great deal of power over you; he or she will be entitled to physical custody of you and may change where you live.

Your conservator, on the other hand, is someone placed in a position of trust with the duty of managing your income, cash, and property. Your conservator will make the decisions regarding all your assets; you will no longer be calling the shots.

Your conservator must always act with your best interest at heart and attempt to take into account your known desires and wishes, but at the end of the day, your conservator, not you, will call the shots.

Your conservator is supposed to provide for your support and care, keep accurate financial records, and submit financial reports, an accounting of how your assets were spent and managed to the court probably at least annually.

Who Gets Appointed

Once the court hears and reviews all the facts, it can decide whether to put an adult guardianship or conservatorship in place, and it will also decide whether the guardianship or conservatorship will be permanent or for a limited period. The court has the discretion to appoint the same person or different people to hold these positions.

You're Not in Control of Who Gets Selected

Guardianships and conservatorships automatically terminate on the death of the ward, you, but after your mental capacity is impaired, the decision about who gets selected will not be within your control. You failed to plan for yourself, so the court will have to do your planning for you.

The person who is appointed as your guardian or conservator or both may be someone you know and trust, or it may be a total stranger, someone you would never have wanted to serve in that role. Keep in mind that a guardian is much like the parent of a child, except in this case, the "child" is you.

If you had planned earlier, while you were still mentally competent to do so, all of this would have been avoided and you would have been able to select your own representative.

The reality here is that you must plan while you can or someone else will force a plan (probably one you won't like) on you.

A Matter of Public Record

The court process, any hearings, and any associated documents dealing with conservatorship or guardianship are all public information. Anyone who wants to see the documents will be able to. You have to decide whether this would be an embarrassment to you or not.

If you are mentally incompetent, you will have no say in keeping your information private. The only way to not have to go through this process is to put proper estate planning documents in place that will allow your family members to act on your behalf and avoid going through the courts to do so.

Compensation

Your guardian and conservator will be compensated for their work by the court, but that compensation will come right out of your money and assets.

The job of a conservator requires lots of paperwork and reporting to the court, and these costs to your estate will probably be large. The cost for doing proper estate planning is minimal compared to the costs of the guardian and conservator. Doing your estate planning now as opposed to having the court do it for you later is much cheaper.

Conservators are paid according to a set, legal schedule. They will receive:

- a 2.5 percent commission on all sums received
- an additional 2.5 percent of all money paid out by the conservator, or 10 percent of all interest earned, whichever the conservator chooses

- an additional .5 percent commission on the market value of the ward's estate

- reimbursement for any expenses

The fees and commission can add up and be a huge drag on your estate. Every dollar paid to your conservator is a dollar your heirs will never receive.

On top of all this, your estate will have to pay the attorney's fees involved.

While guardians and conservators won't become rich serving in these positions, their costs could have easily been avoided if proper estate planning had been done ahead of time.

What Doesn't Work as a Substitute for an Advance Health Care Directive?

- telling your wishes to family members

- a financial power of attorney

- telling your wishes to your physician ahead of time

None of these options give the proper, required, legal authority to anyone to act on your behalf.

Goal: Understanding Alternatives to Adult Guardianship and Conservatorship

You can plan ahead to take advantage of the less-expensive alternatives to guardianship and conservatorship court proceedings. But a consideration much bigger than saving money is what you want to take place if you become mentally incapacitated. The time to decide is now whether you want a probate court making decisions for you or whether you want to be in charge.

Alternatives to Probate Court Proceedings

The alternatives to having a probate court put someone in place to make healthcare and financial decision for you include:

- living trust (with appropriate components)
- advance directive for health care
- durable power of attorney for health care (only older documents*)
- living will (only older documents*)
- financial power of attorney

*The Georgia statute for living wills and durable powers of attorney was repealed effective in 2007. Only those living will and durable power of attorney documents executed prior to the repeal are of any effect.

The newer Advance Directive for Health Care document combines the components of a living will and durable power of attorney for health care into a much better document. I was pleased when the two documents were combined because I was never a fan of the living will document; it was too bare-bones when it came to life-and-death medical decisions.

The Advance Directive for Health Care has all the components of the older durable power, and it allows you to select a person to serve as your guardian if you are suffering from mental incapacity.

When you consider whom to name as your agent to make medical decisions on your behalf if you become unable to do so, you have to consider if the person will stand to benefit financially or otherwise if he or she withholds medical treatment from you.

Making emotional decision such as whether to allow or withhold medical treatment is a very heavy responsibility and can be quite fraught with emotion. Is the person you are considering able to make sound decisions at such a time as that?

When difficult medical decisions must be made, there are often family members present with their own opinions. The agent you select must have enough internal fortitude and be strong enough to fulfill your desires as set out in your planning documents. Is this person able to stand up for you and not be influenced by well-meaning family members who may want something different from what your planning documents require? Can this person ask your doctors intelligent and pertinent questions and not be intimidated by them? Will this person understand what your doctors are saying and be able to think a complicated situation through and then decide, even when there may not be a perfectly clear-cut medical situation?

Will this person be able to make the tough decisions and go to sleep knowing he or she did the very best to honor your true desires? Even if the person you are thinking of has all the above qualifications, this won't matter if he or she lives across the county and cannot be present when you have a medical emergency.

Consideration When Selecting Someone to Serve as your Medical Agent–Will This Person:

- have any financial conflicts of interest?

- be steadfast enough to act in times of great emotion?

- be strong enough to honor your wishes and not be swayed by the emotions or opions of your family members?

- be able to ask doctors probing questions?

- be ablt to evaluate different medical options and options?

- be able to live with the tough decisions he or she may have to make?

- be available in a time of medical emergency?

Goal: Understanding the Importance of Estate Planning

"A good man leaves an inheritance to his children's children."

—Proverbs 13:22 ESV

Estate planning used to be simply about deciding who inherited your estate, but life has become much more complicated than that. In this day of increased life expectancy, it's also come to mean helping protect you and your spouse while you are alive.

It's also about deciding *when* your heirs will receive what you will leave them (immediately or over time) and how you can protect their inheritances so they don't blow them or have them taken away by creditors or during a divorce.

Today's estate planning is about all the death issues, but it's also about all these life issues and more. So instead of considering estate planning as death planning, think of it in terms of acting responsibly and planning for those loved ones you will leave behind. They need you to create a wise plan that will protect what resources God has entrusted to with and pass them on as intact as possible.

The goals of this expanded concept of estate planning should be to:

- relieve your spouse and your children of as much burden as possible. That includes making sure they aren't burdened by:
  - your physical incapacity
  - your mental incapacity
  - having to go through the probate process
  - worrying about whether your assets will be preserved
- protect the inheritance you leave your spouse, children, and grandchildren from predators and unforeseen circumstances

Your Assets are Important, So Plan While You Can

Estate planning isn't just for rich people; it's for regular, middle-class folks such as my parents and millions of others who need to make sure they have the resources to take care of themselves in their later years and still leave as much as possible to their heirs.

Your assets could include money, cars, boats, your home, a second home, CDs, bonds, investments, gold, coins, and family mementos and heirlooms. No matter how small your estate may seem, once you add it all up, it can be considerable, and you'll want your loved ones to get it.

Properly transferring assets and money is not as simple as preparing a simple legal document; it's the result of thoughtful consulting about your most valuable assets—yourself, your spouse, and your family.

Estate planning is a thought process, one that involves thinking through your goals. It's thinking about what you really want for your spouse, your children, and grandchildren. It's about thinking of them in all their specific situations.

It's Never to Early to Plan, But It Can be Too Late to Plan

You've worked very hard your entire life to amass what you own, so you need a game plan for yourself, your spouse, and the other loved ones you'll leave behind. When you're on your deathbed is not the best time to begin the thinking and planning process. You can show your love to your spouse and children by having your estate's legal affairs in order.

Shortly after you die is not when your spouse needs to find out about all the assets you have. You can save your spouse and children a lot of grief at your death, which will be a very tough, emotional time for them, by having planned well in advance.

We all know we can't control the future, but we can make sure we do the very best we can to help the future be as manageable as possible for our families.

Keep Your Assets in Your Family Bloodline

Estate planning helps keep your estate in the family bloodline so you can benefit those you love the most. Think of what your estate can do for your loved ones:

- start them off in life
- help them buy a first home
- encourage them to get or complete a college education
- help them start a business
- provide for a special-needs child or grandchild

The goal is to have your legal affairs arranged so what you leave to your family will do the most good for them. It's never too early to plan—but it's sometimes too late.

Estate planning isn't about paperwork, documents, signatures, or sessions in a lawyer's office; it's about taking care of an important part of this season of life and the responsibility we have to our loved ones. That's as true of me as a husband and a father as it is of you.

No one wants to discuss estate planning, but people do, deep in their hearts, want to put plans in place to accomplish their desires and wishes. Estate planning is how people can indeed accomplish those wishes and desires and pass not only their wealth but also their money to their loved ones.

I put a positive spin on estate planning in this way: think of it like Christmas shopping, except that you already have the presents. We're simply talking about making sure particular gifts get to particular recipients for specific purposes and avoiding trouble (or troublemakers) along the way.

This gift (estate) planning, if you will, is how you're going to avoid the bad things that can happen to your things and loved ones if you have not planned or if you have planned improperly.

Bad Plan 1:
Doing Nothing

Clients have told me, "I don't want to deal with it!" I understand. No one wants to tackle unpleasant tasks, and the fear of dying and dealing with the difficult questions surrounding it can be unpleasant.

Some think that they're not rich enough to need estate planning, but very often, when I've gotten them to sit down and add everything up, they're surprised at the total. And no matter what the total is in your specific case, it still has to be dealt with in an efficient manner for it to be able to accomplish what you would like for your survivors.

If you have no plan in place, that in itself is a plan, and that plan will fail. Estate planning can be likened to eating Brussels sprouts; we must do what is good for us even if it isn't our top choice.

My experience as an estate planner is that it actually can be done in a few short hours if the clients do not procrastinate and buckle down with some discipline.

The alternatives to quality estate planning are not attractive. You can turn a blind eye to the whole matter out of fear or apathy, but doing nothing will never yield satisfactory results for you or your family.

Bad Plan 2:
Thinking Your Planning Was Sufficient

You can also use your limited knowledge of estate planning and cross your fingers that what planning you've done will accomplish what you want it to when the time comes, but the chances of that turning out well are very slim.

Many think they have done all the estate planning they need to do, while others in their hearts know they haven't done proper planning but act as if they have.

Some people's preplanning consists of changing a few bank accounts into joint tenancy and perhaps retitling their homes. (This, by the way, can be disastrous for Medicaid planning).

This type of estate planning is not only very crude estate planning, it is also very dangerous. Relying on making some accounts joint-ownership accounts can have severe, unexpected, and unintended consequences such as loss of control and loss of the assets themselves.

Dangers of Co-Ownership and Joint Tenancy

Joint tenancy has many negative ramifications that folks usually don't see until it's too late; by that time, they've lost control over their assets.

- The folks you give it to don't have to give it back, even if you desperately need it and ask with tears in your eyes.

- Even if they want to give it back, the odds are they have already spent it.

- They don't have to invest it or handle it in the way you'd want them to.

- If they get divorced, their next spouses may have opinions different from yours.

- Their creditors may sue and seize it.

- Their spouses may get it in divorce proceedings.

- They may die before you, and your assets may get passed on to someone else.

- It's not a very flexible planning technique, unlike a will or a living trust.

- They may have to pay more taxes due to the loss in stepped-up cost basis.

- You can't get it back unless the other party agrees to that.

- Your co-owner may not divide the asset(s) among other heirs as you want them to.

- Your tax planning may become complicated or even nullified if you put assets into joint tenancy or co-ownership.

- You will have to get their permission to finance or refinance the asset, and they may decline.

Thinking that this type of "planning" is good estate planning is a huge mistake.

You'll Receive a Test Score—From Your Loved Ones

The way you conduct your life is *not* a rehearsal for the real event; your life is the real event, and you will be given a passing or failing grade by those you love.

If you ignore sound advice and fail to plan, there is good news and bad news. The good news is that you won't have to worry about getting your test score because you'll have already died. The bad news is that your loved ones may have to suffer with the consequences of your not doing what you should have done to receive a passing grade.

Goal: Understanding Probate: A Time-Consuming, Stressful Job at the Worst Possible Time

"For where a will is involved, the death of the one who
made it must be established."

—Hebrews 9:16 (NASB)

What is Probate?

Simply put, probate is the court process required to take your assets from your name and put them into the names of your heirs, and to allow anyone the opportunity to challenge your will. Generally speaking, probate should be (and can be) avoided, but it depends on your individual situation.

The probate process, regardless of how large or complex your estate is, still takes time and money at the worst possible time—at your death, when your spouse and children are least willing and able to deal with something like this. Why ask your loves ones to have to deal with court processes at that time?

Probate has its negatives: it will occur at the worst possible time for your loves ones, especially your spouse. It will be a frustrating process complicated by the grief they will feel, and their minds won't be in the game at all. We all know that the worst time to do anything is when it has to be done immediately.

Dealing with Probate Ahead of Time

Why can't we deal with this ahead of time? We can—with a living trust. The chief advantage to a living trust is that both spouses will be present as it is being crafted, but in addition, it will be done at a time of much less stress for the person who will ultimately be the survivor.

Goal: Using the Right Tools for the Right Job

Tools to Accomplish Your Desires

Estate planning is mostly about expert consulting combined with a wise use of proper tools to accomplish a client's goals and safeguarding the client from pitfalls he or she may not have known about.

I encourage you to not worry so much about which tools will be used and instead simply focus on what your wishes and desires are as well as considering what pitfalls you want to avoid.

Each client's situation is different. Once an experienced estate planning attorney knows what your goals are, he or she will be in the best position to determine what tools are best to use in your specific situation.

Documents for Life as well as Death

You may not realize it, but some estate planning documents are good for only while you're alive. Once you die, they no longer have any effect, and other documents will take over.

An enhanced financial power of attorney and an advance health care directive are examples of documents that apply to you when you're living.

After you've died, documents that had no effect when you were alive will become active and used to arrange your affairs the way you wanted them to be arranged. A will is a good example of a document that comes into play only after death.

Some documents, however, can function before and after your death. These include:

- Living Trusts
- Medicaid Asset Protection Trusts
- Asset Protection Trusts

It is important that you realize the time frames of all such documents and how they will help you achieve your estate planning goals.

Estate Planning Tools

My dad always told me, "Cheap tools aren't worth it." Cheap tools are cheap for a reason. They may look very similar to those of higher quality on the shelf, but anyone who has used cheap and more-expensive tools will be quick to tell you that once you put them to work, their differences quickly become apparent. You find that the cheap tool just won't get the job done, and you realize you wasted your money and will have to buy the quality tool anyway.

You may not enjoy paying the higher price for quality tools right from the start, but you will know it will get the job done, and it will save you money in the long run.

"Fill in the Blank" Documents

You can find a "$20 Will Kit" or a "$100 Trust Kit" in any office supply store or even many places online. But how do you know that $20 will kit or a $100 trust kit is really worth what you pay for them? What would you think if their real cost ended up being $8,000?

If you're buying a document but don't really know if it's suitable for the job you need it for, it may do more harm than good. How much will it cost to deal with the mess it may cause when it ultimately doesn't deal with your assets the way you thought it was supposed to?

Is your and your family's peace of mind worth only $100? Are you willing to save a relatively small sum for your estate planning at the risk that everything you've worked hard for your life will be taken care of by that cheap will kit or trust kit?

The problem is that one-size-fits-all documents don't fit anyone properly. Cookie-cutter documents are a "hope" plan in that you hope they will accomplish your goals, but you will never know if they will or not; they will come into play only after you are dead. Your family may have to pay the price for you using cheap tools.

Goal: Understanding the Different Kinds of Wills

There are many different types of wills.

- single-person will

- testamentary trust will

- pour-over will

- holographic will

- oral will (aka noncupative will)

- joint will

- defective will

- living will (not a real will at all)

- intestacy (not a real will at all, but a bad Georgia will substitute plan)

A Special Category: Outdated Wills

I'll list separately an unfortunate category of wills, and that is the outdated will.

Many issues may make a will outdated. Sometimes, it's because federal tax laws for capital gains or step-ups in basis issues change, or maybe Georgia has a law change or major overhaul to portions of its legal code.

Other reasons a will may be outdated may be "life" issues such as family feuds and needing to change a bequest but forgetting to among them.

Having a will that has become outdated will likely not result in you accomplishing your desires for the distribution of your assets to your loved ones. Worse still, it may cause a result that is the exact opposite of what you would have wanted.

This is why you should have your will reviewed every so often, with every three years being a good bench mark.

Surprise Category: Unintentionally Revoked Wills

Georgia law requires that your existing will be revoked if you later marry, remarry, have a child, or adopt a child. If any of these events is about to happen, you need to immediately, before the event, have your will reviewed. The will may be alright and not need to be rewritten, but it may need changes made. It is far more preferable that you don't wait until after any of these events occurred, although your will can still be reviewed and may be alright or can be rewritten quickly.

Goal: Understanding the Different Parts of a Will

A will is a technical legal document. It may appear to be just a bunch of words to those who aren't attorneys, but a will must have all its parts present and accounted for.

What goes into a will? Important parts of a will:

- How your creditors will be paid (your life stops but your debts live)
- Funeral arrangements
- Bequests
    - particular
    - general
    - universal
- Naming executor or executrix
    - coexecutor
    - alternate executor
- Testamentary trusts (only take effect at death)
    - trustee

- o beneficiaries
- Guardians of minor children
  - o same person as executor, or different?
  - o Same person as trustee, or different?
- Survivorship clause
- Collation provision
- Disposition of personal effects
- Executor's powers
- Proper signature block
- Proper number of signatures
- Witness block
- Proper number of witnesses
- Self-proving document

This is the mere list of the parts of a will. It is beyond the scope of this book, which is aimed at laypeople, to lay out how each part should be written and how to avoid any conflicts between the different parts, for example, an executor and a trustee or the payment of debts versus different beneficiaries.

Goal: Understanding that a Will is a Tool

Wills Take Effect Only Upon Death

A very important principle to understand is that a will is a document that doesn't take effect until your death; while you're alive, your will doesn't do anything.

Some people mistakenly think that a will transfers some ownership rights immediately when it is created, but it doesn't.

Some people also think that a will provides for other needs they have, such as for a financial power of attorney or health care power of attorney or directive, but it doesn't.

A will is only an "at death" planning document; it doesn't solve any of the problems you may encounter before death, such as mental incapacity. It also can't incorporate several powerful and needed documents such as financial power of attorney or a health care power of attorney, but a trust might be able to include these.

Pros and Cons of Wills

There are several positives to the creation of a will as compared to another type of document.

- They can sometimes be less expensive (at least initially, but not once the costs of probate are added).

- They are a more familiar document to you than say, for example, a living trust.

Wills, however, have some negatives that may outweigh their positives when compared to alternatives, such as living trusts. Before you decide on a will instead of a living trust, get some expert advice and a thorough review of your specific situation and goals.

- Wills may not be the cheapest over the long haul (once you include costs of probate).

- Wills must go through the probate process.

- The will probate process will happen at the worst possible time for your family.

- Wills don't protect you from nursing home costs.

- Wills don't protect you from disability or adult guardianship.

- Wills don't protect you from former spouses, children's broken marriages, or any of your heirs' immature or irresponsible behavior.

- Any type of trust set up in a will (called a testamentary trust) doesn't take effect until your death.

Simple Wills

Most people think the will they're considering creating is a "simple" will. While there are certainly wills that are simple and basic, the goals you want to accomplish with your estate, along with the type of assets you have and the family and beneficiaries issues you have, may not in reality end up being as "simple" as you think it could be.

Joint Wills

Some people try to save money by creating joint wills with their spouses, but this is not really an effective cost-savings measure. To craft a joint will requires careful attention to the details and can sometimes end up being confusing to the executor of the estate of either spouse.

If changes must be made to a joint will at a later date, that can get a little more involved as well; both spouses will be required to sign the new version of the joint will.

Required Formalities of a Will in Georgia

For a will to be valid under Georgia law, it must comply with certain minimum formalities. Beware: will "kits" that you can get online or at office supply stores are "generic" forms that may not meet all the formalities of Georgia law and as a result may not be valid.

In addition, generic will forms are "fill-in-the-blank" types of documents. If you make mistakes when you work with them, you may accidentally end up doing something with your assets you didn't want to.

If the will is found to be invalid, your estate will be handled as if you had died without a will, or "intestate." The problem with dying intestate is that the wishes and desires you put into your invalid, fill-in-the-blank document will be ignored, and your assets will be distributed according to Georgia laws of intestacy.

Words Matter

There's another problem with fill-in-the-blank wills—their wording. Sometimes, they incorporate generic, boilerplate wording that people who aren't experienced estate planning lawyers, won't recognize as contrary to fulfilling your estate planning goals, which may result in a disaster.

Simple examples of this are the use of the phrases "my husband" or "my children"; these phrase are not specific enough, and in certain circumstances, their inclusion in your will may result in your assets going to the wrong person.

Will kits and trust kits are often not detailed enough, but this can escape the eyes of a layperson not knowledgeable about how much detail should be included in a will. For example, if you mention too few details in the will's bequests section, it may be difficult for anyone else to understand what you wanted. It may be easy for you to understand now, but you won't be around to explain matters when your will is probated.

In addition, as contrary as this may sound, sometimes you may actually mention too many details.

How to Handle Personal Property

While some people may say they want their real estate split up equally, it's a different story when it comes to personal property.

Nearly everyone has personal property they want to go to a specific heir, and there are two ways to handle this. One is legally nonbinding; it may not ensure your property gets to the person you want it to get to. Another type is legally binding, and it will ensure the right person gets the right item.

These different methods have their pros and cons, so it's very important that you discuss the two ways with an experienced estate planning attorney.

Testamentary Trusts: Special Trusts Inside a Will

I have mentioned that some of the estate planning tools available are wills, living trusts, other kinds of trusts, and other documents that are used during your mental incapacity.

Wills can actually have trusts set up inside them. The difference between a trust set up inside a will and a trust set up by itself (or inside a living trust) is that the trust inside a will doesn't take effect until you die, whereas the other kinds of trusts take effect usually during your life (called *inter vivos* trusts).

Depending on what your objective is for any particular trust, an individual trust may best be a testamentary trust or an *inter vivos* (for example, a living trust).

Importance of Residuary Clauses

If you have items you don't specifically list in your will to be given to this or that beneficiary, or if you don't list them as part of a general category of assets (i.e., "personal property"), those items may have to be handled as if you had died without a will ("intestate") for just those items, and the court will decide how to handle them.

The same goes for a specific asset you wanted to go to a specific person who happens to have died before you.

The way to avoid this problem is to include a residuary clause in your will that handles these types of items in ways you select yourself rather than having Georgia laws of intestacy rule for these items only.

How to Choose an Executor

If you and your estate planning attorney decide that drafting a will is more suitable than a trust for your situation, a very important decision you will make is who will serve as the will's executor.

This is an important decision because you will not be around to supervise whether your executor does what he or she is supposed to do and in a reasonably quick manner.

If the executor you pick doesn't take action quickly to probate your estate, months, even years, may pass. If he or she doesn't know the steps to take or doesn't hire an estate planning attorney, you can just about guarantee that the process will take a very long time.

A horror story told to me the other day by someone I met was that the executor of his mother's estate had hired a young attorney to probate his mother's will, but the attorney had filed incorrect probate paper work three separate times. Yes, three separate times. Months and months had been wasted, and he and his family are still no closer to getting their loves one's affairs taken care of.

The person you choose to be your executor should be honest, stable, able to think, and unconcerned with what the rest of the family thinks.

Alternative Executors

Some people asked to be executors refuse to take the job because they decide they wouldn't be able to handle the pressure or think they won't have the time to deal with the probate process. This is why you must also select alternative executors.

Why Some Wills Sit in Limbo (Aren't Probated) for Years, Even Decades

Many estates don't get probated for years and years. While at first this may not make sense, the reason for this is that most laypeople simply don't want to get involved with any process that involves a court. The result is that properties aren't transferred to their correct new owners and that other important tasks are left undone.

Delayed Probate can Result in "Double Probate"

Sometimes, a delay in getting an estate probated can be so long that one of the will's beneficiaries dies. The property this beneficiary was supposed to inherit was therefore never titled in his or her name but is now supposed to be transferred to that person's beneficiaries (probably the grandchildren of the first deceased person). That will not happen until the first will is probated.

Fear of the probate process, fear of having to deal with the court, and fear of having to hire an attorney are some of the reasons for some executors' extreme delays in handling this big responsibility. A living trust would have avoided all this delay.

Don't Let Just Anyone Sign as Witness to Your Will

Sometimes, when you meet at an attorney's office to sign a will, a mistake is made—the wrong person or persons are asked to witness the signing of the will.

Your attorney should be experienced enough to know that certain people shouldn't be allowed to witness the signing of the will. While this is basic stuff, I have experienced such lapses firsthand— an "experienced" attorney who created a grandmother's will allowed her son to sign it. This was a big mistake.

It was a mistake because the son was a named a beneficiary in the will. This could have led to a sticky probate process in which he would have had to forfeit his share of the will; his share would pass through the residuary clause, just as if the grandmother had died intestate. The court would decide what to do with what was supposed to go to the son.

Safeguarding Your Estate Planning Documents

Once you've finished your estate planning and have your customized documents in hand, the next question is, "What do I do with them?"

Whatever location you select for the documents has to meet three goals:

- it must keep the documents from getting accidentally lost

- it must be known by and accessible to your executor

- it must be protected from being destroyed by an heir who doesn't like the will.

Below are some ideas as to where to safekeep your estate documents, some traditional, some less so:

- wherever you store your important papers (a lockable file cabinet or safe too big to be carried off

- safety deposit box

- attorney's office

- probate court vault or safe (you can log it in and let executor know he or she can access it at the time of your death)

Each of these options has advantages and disadvantages, so speak with an experienced estate planning attorney to discuss the best place for you.

Copies of Your Documents

Should you keep copies of your signed original planning documents? Attorneys will differ in their opinions on this, but my answer is no—don't keep copies of the signed originals. It's difficult enough for some folks to remember where their one will or trust is much more two different copies. Your documents should already be in a safe place.

What you don't want to happen is to change your document's language but at your death have a relative find an earlier version of the will. This may lead to confusion at best and a challenge to the will at worst. This is one of the reasons many attorneys favor living trusts instead of wills.

Years Later, Your Witnesses Can't Be Found

Signing the will is not a casual process. Everything about signing the will and the way the witnesses are supposed to sign the will and what they sign can have a tremendous effect on that future event in the life of every will, the probate.

When the executor begins the probate process, he or she will quickly find that at least one possible step has been avoided if the attorney who drafted the will used certain language that made it unnecessary to find the witnesses and get them to sign probate documents, which is otherwise a necessity.

This can be important since oftentimes, years and years have passed since the will was signed. Your executor may not be able to find the witnesses to the will signing. They may be dead, or have moved, or simply cannot be found.

Don't let this hinder the probate process; take advantage of the knowledge of an experienced attorney to make sure your will isn't held up because your witnesses can't be found.

Selecting and Executor:
Important Things to Think

- Don't pick someone simply because you like him or her.

- Is the person honest?

- Will the person actually do the job when it comes time?

- Will the person be too slow with the probate process?

- Is this person intimidated by legal matters?

- Will this person be too affected by your death to dothe job correctly and diligently?

- Will the person have the time for all the paperwork required?

- Is this person intelligent enough to do the job?

Goal: Avoiding Challenges to Your Will

Someone in the crowd said to Him [Jesus], "Teacher, tell
my brother to divide the inheritance with me." But He
said to him, "Man, who made me a judge or arbitrator
over you?"

And He [Jesus] said to them, "Take care, and be on your
guard against all covetousness, for one's life does not
consist in the abundance of his possessions."

—Luke 12:13–15 ESV

Professionally Drafted Documents Help Prevent Family Quarrels

"Take care, and be on your guard against all covetousness," the
Bible verse above says. Covetousness is all around us. People lust
for more than they have, and they lust for more than their "fair"
shares.

Frequently, when they think the shares they've received aren't "fair," they take action to fix that. This is how a probate court will contest gets started.

Covetousness has been around a long time. In this biblical account, someone was trying to force his brother to probate his father's will. We're not sure what else was going on, but perhaps he was trying to get a share of an estate his father had cut him out of, or perhaps he was trying to get more of the estate.

Whatever the reason, he was looking for someone who would agree with him.

His next action was probably to file a challenge to the will in Jerusalem's equivalent of a probate court.

Family Feuds

Your children may seem perfectly content today. You may find it impossible to believe they would ever disagree about anything associated with your will, particularly the wishes you have expressed in it.

However, I caution you to never assume everyone will be happy with what your will says. After you're dead and gone, your heirs' true, raw feelings will arise about any number of issues, including how you gave your money away when you were alive as compared to the way your money is being split up by your will.

No everyone will share your opinion that the situation is "fair." Siblings often think and strongly feel, rightly or wrongly, that their sisters or brothers received more than was "fair" when taking into consideration all the past events in the family's history. A family feud is an ugly sight, especially when it's over a will, but it happens a lot more often than you'd think.

Don't think that your will won't be challenged or contested just because you feel the dollars at stake are small or you know those to whom you are leaving it well. Money, sometimes even in small amounts, can bring out the worst in people, especially if they feel they've been slighted or ill-treated. This is an important reason to carefully consider how to divide money and assets up between children. If they believe an injustice has been done, they are much more likely to feel they have nothing to lose and file a challenge to the will. The last thing you will ever want to do is leave a legacy of contention.

This is another reason trusts win hands down when compared to wills. If you use a living trust, you don't have to worry about it being challenged in probate court, but that's not to say you shouldn't strongly consider the issues of fairness and "equality" I've discussed elsewhere in this book.

Setting a will up, at the beginning, to avoid any challenge is important because even if a will challenge is defeated, the cost in money, time, and emotional energy can be very high, and your heirs will have to wait months or years longer before they receive their share of your estate. Sometimes, families never recover from the emotions resulting from such an event.

Who Can File a Challenge?

Who can challenge your will? The short answer is *anyone*. The more-correct answer is any interested person. The challenger doesn't have to be your heir. Pretty amazing, isn't it?

Challenging a Will Is Shockingly Easy

Challenging a will can take many forms, but the simplest form a challenge takes is when an heir refuses to sign the probate documents in spite of repeated requests. This causes the probate process to grind to a halt and the legal fees to climb; the attorney will have to spend more time dealing with any noncooperative heir. The attorney may even have to file a probate court motion to get the case moving ahead.

Grounds for Challenging a Will

The way the will is signed, the way it is initialed, and the way it is witnessed and signed by the witnesses can all have huge effects on whether someone might challenge the will. There are numerous grounds for challenging a will, including failure to follow required formalities, incapacity, freedom of volition, fraud, undue influence, misrepresentation, and mistakes.

Failure to Follow Required Formalities

To protect the person creating the will and to help ensure his or her desires are fulfilled, the law requires certain formalities be followed not to create difficulties but to protect that person from frivolous challenges to the will. These formalities, however, help only if they are followed to a T. The formalities include signing (known as "executing") the will properly and attesting it properly.

The will should be properly witnessed. There is a danger when the will is not witnessed at all or when too few witnesses were used. Another danger is when the wrong witnesses are used—by that I mean witnesses who are beneficiaries of the will.

The more of these formalities there are that are not done or not done properly, the greater the chance that someone could challenge the will.

Parts Left Out of a Will

A will is a legal document that needs certain parts to actually be a will, and it needs certain parts to fulfill its desired function.

It is important for a will to be "clean" to glide through probate with no hassle, but this won't be the case when certain "parts" are left out, for instance, a residuary clause. Not having one could tie up some of your assets and make the matter, as to those assets, as if you had died intestate, without a will.

Wills that do not include a self-proving document could be subject to delay, greater costs, and a greater likelihood of being challenged.

A Will Not Properly Drafted

If the will is not properly drafted, it may be open to a challenge. A will not drafted competently or not clear in its intentions may leave the probate court not knowing exactly what the will directs the executor to do. If the will is confusing or unclear, or if there are conflicts in what it says, someone may challenge it.

Use of Improper or Unclear Phrases

One example of a confusing or unclear phrase is when people or property are mentioned too generally. An example could be "my house" when the person who wrote the will has more than one. Perhaps one house has a debt on it and the other doesn't; a beneficiary supposed to get a house with debt might challenge the will, wanting to receive the one with no debt.

Other problems can be caused by unclear wording; your intentions for the disposition of your property might be clear but the language isn't. "My sister's husband," for instance, could be confusing if your sister had divorced and remarried between the time you made your will and you died. She will have a husband, but will that be the husband you originally intended to name in your will?

Use of improper phrases can cause problems as well. For instance, "It is my wish that ..." is much too ambiguous of a phrase. Do you mean you are simply asking nicely that something be done, that you don't require your executor to do this particular thing, that it's up to his or her discretion?

Writing a Will by Yourself

Wills written by individuals without competent help from an attorney will usually fail to follow the formalities, and that will make them more prone to challenges. The more formalities they fail to follow, the greater the likelihood a challenge will be successful; there will be that many more grounds on which challenges can be mounted.

These are my reasons for strongly suggesting no one rely on an oral or a handwritten will (a *holographic* will). These forms of wills are just asking for trouble in so many different ways.

Lack of Sound Mind

The later in life someone puts off getting a will done, the greater the chance that someone else will raise this factor as a challenge to the will. An older will maker might have shaky handwriting, and this in itself may encourage someone to challenge it.

Cognitive Issues

If you are beginning to have mental or cognitive issues, the risk that your will may be challenged goes way up. The problem for you is that since it's your brain that may be failing, you probably won't even recognize that it's happening, but others will.

Worse yet, if you begin to have cognitive issues, that might make it too late for you to create a reliable will at all.

Undue Influence

Another problem with waiting to creating a well crafted estate plan is that the longer you wait, the older you get. And the older you get, the likelihood is greater that someone will actually have what is called "undue influence" over you or that someone will allege that someone else had undue influence over you. If you begin suffering from cognitive issues, someone exerting undue influence could be a real danger.

Multiple Copies of a Will

It is not unusual for a person to change a will as the years go by, but a problem can arise when previous versions of the will are not completely revoked or destroyed.

If heirs find older wills that are more favorable to them, they may attempt to challenge the newer will on any number of grounds.

This issue can also arise when codicils are used to amend or change wills rather than simply creating entirely new wills.

Others Reasons

Other grounds on which someone may challenge your will include:

- Claim of republication of a will

- Fraud

- Mistake

You must not ignore the possibility of challenges to your will. Just because you think there are no grounds doesn't mean there are none or that they won't come up later. Not only that—even if turns out that there are no legitimate bases to challenge your will, they still must be dealt with in probate court, and that will cause delay and increased attorney's fees.

You should consider using certain estate planning tools that greatly reduce the opportunities for anyone to challenge your estate plan. An experienced estate planning attorney can explain these to you and help you know if they are right for your circumstances.

Goal: Understanding Trusts

What is a trust? Think of it as a container, a box. Some trusts are revocable, while others are irrevocable, but they all share certain components.

Five Parts of a Trust

A trust has five basic components.

- Trust maker (also called the grantor, trustor, or settlor)
- Trustee
- Beneficiaries
- Corpus (assets in the trust)
- Terms of the trust

Trust Maker

The trust maker (aka grantor, trustor, settlor) is the person who sets the trust up and transfers assets into it.

Trustee

The trustee is the party or person to whom the assets are deeded. For instance, one could be titled "John Smith, Trustee for the John Smith Family Trust."

The trustee is a person with the responsibility of taking care of the assets in the trust and doing with them only what the terms of the trust allow the trustee to do.

The settlor can serve as the trustee in certain circumstances, as can the beneficiaries.

Beneficiaries

The beneficiaries are those who will receive benefit from the trust; they are the reason the trust was created. The trust gives the beneficiaries legal rights set out and explained in the trust document.

Terms of the Trust

What are the goals of the settlor? They are contained in the clauses of the trust. They tell the trustee how he or she is supposed to administrate the trust and the duties the position entails. The clauses also tell the beneficiaries what benefits they will receive and when.

The clauses are the "rules" the trust is run by; they are how everyone knows if the trust is being administered properly. For this reason, all trust clauses should be specific, not generic. They must be understandable by the settlor, the trustee, and the beneficiaries alike.

Corpus—The Trust's Assets

After a trust is designed, and all its terms and clauses carefully written, the settlor will transfer assets into it that will be managed by the trustee on behalf of the beneficiaries.

Important Matters to Consider When Selecting a Trustee–Is He or She:

- Trustworthy?

- Knowledgeable of money besides knowing how to spend it?

- Realize what being a "fiducidary" means?

- Experienced in holding positions of responsiblility?

- Able to interact with but be independent of those he or she will have interation with i.e., brokers, bankers, ect.?

- Experienced in managing sums of money similar to those he or she will have to manage in the trust?

- Free of conflicts of interest with you or with your goals of the trust?

Goal: Making Sure Your Trust Does What You Want It To

A trust is a tool created by crafting very specialized legal documents. In spite of the fact that there are so many lawyers out there, very few truly know their way around these very sophisticated tools.

You must be very careful about choosing someone to draft a trust for you. Some naive practitioners, not knowing any better or even not caring, will use plain, generic, one-size-fits-all, cookie-cutter documents. Such noncustomized documents may appear to be alright simply because they can certainly look like legal documents, but looks can be deceiving, especially when it comes to legal documents.

All Trusts are Not Equal

All trusts are not equal. Just because a document says "Trust" at the top and has legal-looking text doesn't mean it will accomplish what you want.

Those who think all trusts are equal will buy estate planning help based only on price. They don't realize they need wise, experienced, and quality legal counsel, not merely a handful of good-looking documents.

A trust is a sophisticated, specialized legal document. I want to be brutally honest here: generic trusts are a waste of time and money, and worse than that, they are truly dangerous in that they could end up doing you and your beneficiaries more harm than good.

It's for this reason that inexpensive, off-the-shelf trusts may end up being the most expensive trusts of all. When the time comes for you to rely on your estate planning documents to perform the tasks you intended them to and they fail you, the costs you, or your family after you're deceased, will incur to try to fix things will be much greater than what you saved by buying the discount-priced documents—buyer beware.

Purposes and Benefits of a Trust

A trust is a truly amazing document. It can accomplish many goals, many more than a will can. A trust is a "goal-achievement" vehicle. If you know what goals you want to achieve, a trust can usually get the job done.

Some of the purposes or benefits that folks often use a trust for are to:

- protect assets for minor children
- protect assets for adult children
    - who can't manage money
    - who are credit risks
    - who are at risk of divorce
    - who are irresponsible or wasteful
    - who are immature
    - who are not financially savvy

- protect assets for special-needs people

Customization

A trust document is the best tool to use to help protect your family over the long haul. You don't have to settle for a generic, off-the-shelf trust—you can design a trust just the way you want it, so never settle for less than that. Your family's needs are unique, so your estate planning documents must be unique as well.

Kinds of Trusts

A trust is simply a container, but a very special container that comes with an instruction book that controls and protects how the assets inside the container can be used. Pretty neat, huh?

Sometimes, estate planners refer to these containers as buckets, boxes, or little wagons that you place your assets in. All of these words and phrases are helpful ways to think of trusts.

There are different kinds of trusts. Some have unique names, but all share the same basic characteristics and components. At its heart, a trust is a specialized, customized set of legal documents crafted to best reach the goals you are seeking to achieve. Trusts fall into two major groups, revocable and irrevocable.

Revocable Trusts

Revocable trusts are kind of like boxes with an open top. This means your assets can be added or taken out at any time, and the trust document can be changed almost anytime. They go by several different names. You may have heard them called:

- Revocable Living Trust

- Probate Avoidance Trust
- Will Substitute Trust
- Living Trust
- Loving Trust

These powerful documents can do much, much more than help you avoid probate, which is a great goal in itself; they can also be designed to help you and your family deal with:

- your mental or physical incapacity
- protecting your spouse from gold diggers after you are deceased
- protecting your children who cannot manage money
- protecting your children who have bad marriages
- protecting children who have credit problems
- and many other uses.

Irrevocable Trusts

Irrevocable trusts are boxes that have a closed top for the simple reason of keeping bad people out.

These types of trusts can be used to protect your children and grandchildren from their bad decisions and the bad decisions of others that may impact them.

These trusts can be designed to accomplish many specialized asset protection goals. Different kinds of irrevocable trusts include:

- Asset Protection Trust
- Children's Trust (Minors' Trust)

- Discretionary Trust (also known as a Pot Trust)

- Single Child Trust

- Grandchildren's Trust (also known as a Dynasty Trust)

- Incentive Trust

- Insurance Trust

- Medicaid Asset Protection Trust (also known as a Nursing Home Trust)

- Multiple Children's Trust

- Special-Needs Trust

- Spendthrift Trust

- Sprinkle Trust (also known as a Spray Trust)

- Support Trust

For a more in-depth discussion of trusts and whether one or the other is right or best for your situation, consult with an experienced estate planning attorney.

Goal: Getting in the Habit of Reviewing Your Will

You should review each of your estate planning documents on a regular basis. I know that doesn't sound like much fun, but it's like painting your house or changing your car's oil; it's something that has to be done. Houses aren't meant to never be repainted, and autos aren't meant to never have their oil changed. Bad things may result.

How often should you review your will? I recommend to you that you do so at least every three years and more often if there are law changes or changes in your life or family situation. These include, for instance, if

- you sell real estate listed in your will

- you buy new real estate

- you give away or sell important personal property

- you incur significant or long-term debt that could affect the equity picture of assets given to different heirs and make their bequests different

- you need to change the executor (the person moves away, grows too old, doesn't want to serve, or you are no longer friends)

- you move to a different state

- your health drastically changes

- you decide to change guardianship issues

- your guardians move away, get to old to fulfill their duties, or simply no longer want to serve

- your children have grown, become adults, and change their circumstances

- this or that beneficiary becomes more—or less— responsible

- you want to add beneficiaries

- you want to remove beneficiaries (in case of death or disinheritance)

- you want or need to change how much is distributed to whom

This list is not meant to be exhaustive, but it nevertheless gives you an idea of what kinds of things should prompt you to contact your estate planning attorney.

Goal: Changing Your Will after You Change Your Mind

A will can easily be changed. There are basically two ways a will can be changed. One is to draft another will, and the other is to draft a codicil.

Both methods will do the job, but both can cause problems for you when the time to probate comes.

Method 1:
Creating a Codicil

A codicil is just a written document that fulfills the formalities of a will but is not a will. A codicil is kind of like a "change order" you might give your contractor during a remodeling project. The codicil is a document you can use to add, alter, or delete parts of your will.

A codicil to a will is usually much shorter than the will itself. Years ago, before computers came into general use in law offices, it was much easier to simply create a codicil rather than make changes to an original will and type the whole thing again.

Method 2:
Creating a New Will

Nowadays, computers make it easy to make changes to a will, insert them where they should go in the original document, and punch out a new copy. It's just as easy now to create a new will (or trust, or other legal document) as it is to simply create a codicil, and that's why I consider it unnecessary to utilize a codicil.

A danger of relying on a codicil rather than a rewritten will is that you'll end up with two documents that reflect your wishes, so two documents that you will have to keep careful track of. If the codicil is lost, the old will is all there will be left, and whatever it says will have to be followed.

Change Your Will:
Change, then Revoke

It takes two steps to change your will; both have to be done perfectly to avoid trouble when your will gets to the probate stage.

How to Revoke a Will

There are a number of ways to revoke your will. The goal is to make it so that the older document no longer exists or situated so no one would think that it to be your will. Revocation methods include:

- Obliteration
- Destruction
- Implied
- Express

Events That Automatically Revoke Your Will

While we are talking about changing or revoking a will, be aware that certain life circumstances may revoke your will without your doing it on your own. You can stop this from happening if your will is drafted in such a manner as to stop these from impacting it. Automatic revocation can be caused by:

- subsequent marriage

- subsequent divorce or annulment

- subsequent birth of a child

- subsequent adoption of a child

If any of these events are going to happen in the near future or have happened recently, immediately contact an experienced estate planning attorney.

Goal: Seeing a Living Trust as a Tool

To accomplish your life and your death estate planning goals, you need a quality plan. An experienced estate planning attorney will talk with you about a number of tools, including a versatile living trust.

What is a Living Trust?

A living trust is a trust created during your life. It is like an open box in that you can place money and assets in it and take them out when you want.

It is very popular because of its ability to avoid the probate step that wills have to go through, but that's just the icing on the cake. It can give you control and protection safeguards for your estate after you are gone. Think of it as a will on steroids.

Positives and Negatives

Living trusts are popular because they are like the Swiss army knife of estate planning. They can be greatly customized and must be customized to accomplish your specific family goals.

The pros of living trusts are that they

- are revocable (you can take assets out of them at any time)
- are likely to be less expensive over the long haul than a will
- can deal with future mental disability issues
- can deal with family problems and changes such as former spouses, broken marriages, immaturity, or irresponsibility

The cons of living trusts are that they

- are initially sometimes a little more expensive than a will but are likely to be less expensive over the long haul
- require a little upkeep if new assets have to be placed (named) in the trust, but wills may also have to be changed if your circumstances change in certain ways.

No estate planning tool is perfect; all of them have pros and cons. The goal is to select the right tool, take into consideration whatever cons it has, and customize it to accomplish your goals.

Common Mistakes with Revocable Living Trusts

Most of the mistakes with living trusts are caused either by inexperienced or unsophisticated estate planning attorneys or by the consumers themselves. Mistakes by lower trained estate planning attorneys include

- creating a trust that too generic to accomplish your goals
- failing to completely fund the trust

Mistakes by consumers include

- buying an "off the shelf" trust, trust kit, or forms kit
- failing to fund the trust correctly
- hiring a lawyer to create a "cheap" trust for you that is too generic to accomplish your goals.

Accomplish Your Goals

The whole point of estate planning is so that you can achieve your goals, whether they include encouraging your children or grandchildren to get higher education, to help them buy their first home and so on. It's also about helping you plan for a possible move to a nursing home.

Whatever your goals are, one of the key decisions will be selecting the right tool to achieve them. A living trust can be a powerful tool working for you if it is the right choice for your situation.

Goal: Protecting Assets from Nursing Home Expenses

Doctors are performing miracles these days in keeping us alive so much longer than in past generations, but that could mean that you end up where you don't want to be, in a nursing home and living with a deteriorating body.

As we age, our bodies lose their ability to handle daily activities; they can degrade to the point that we no longer have the ability to perform what it takes to function every day, the activities of daily living (ADLs).

It's not just our bodies that can deteriorate. Our brains can also begin to fail us. Even if our bodies remain strong, our brains may not be able to properly control our bodies.

Don't Ignore the Aging Process

Many people would prefer to remain healthy and active and simply die in their sleep, but the odds of that happening are quite low.

No one likes to think about it, but ignoring how our bodies and minds age and the ramifications of that doesn't make the issue go away.

Once you're no longer able to perform most of the activities of daily living for yourself, you will need a lot of assistance on a daily, perhaps even an hourly, basis.

A nursing home can provide a great deal of care ranging from routine nursing care, assistance with bathing and grooming, feeding, handling medications, helping you get around, and even offering physical, speech, and occupational therapies.

Nursing Home Cost

Nursing homes can provide much assistance, but it all comes at a price, a high price, one that can be financially crushing. Only the truly wealthy can afford to pay out an extra $60,000 to $90,000 a year without having that seriously impact their finances.

Three Ways to Pay

There are only three ways to pay for nursing home health care costs:

- out of pocket
- long-term care insurance
- Medicaid

You'll notice that Medicare is *not* on that list; Medicare simply doesn't pay for custodial nursing home care. It pays only for a very limited amount of short-term care in a nursing home in limited instances, which we'll deal with next.

Why Doesn't Medicare Pay for Nursing Home Care?

Medicare doesn't cover your long-term nursing home stay because it is more like health insurance than long-term care insurance.

Medicare will pay for a very limited number of days in a nursing home facility but only if your health is improving. If your health situation isn't improving, Medicare won't cover your nursing home bills.

In order for Medicare to cover even the limited number of days in a nursing home it does cover, you must:

- have been hospitalized for necessary inpatient care for at least three consecutive days

- have been admitted to a nursing home within thirty days after the date of discharge from the hospital

- need skilled nursing or rehabilitative care on a daily basis for the condition for which you were hospitalized

- receive a physician's order that such care is necessary.

The skilled care that Medicare will pay for (albeit for a very limited time) is different from the longer-term custodial care a nursing home usually provides. Medicare will pay for the former but not the latter.

Even when Medicare pays for skilled care (not custodial care), it will only pay for a maximum of 100 days during any benefit period.

If you have a problem with performing your activities of daily living (ADLs, which include eating, bathing, dressing, toileting, preparing meals, etc.), these types of issues usually aren't going to just get better over time.

Only you can answer whether you can afford the high cost of nursing home care. If you can, you are blessed.

If you can't pay out of your own pocket, you have only two options, Medicaid or long-term care insurance, to which we'll turn next.

Goal: Learning the Facts of Medicaid

Most of What You've Heard about Medicaid Is Incorrect

Medicaid is a federal program administered by individual states; there is no federal "Department of Medicaid" to look to regarding Medicaid eligibility.

While there are many similarities among the rules in different states, there are many differences as well; the way Medicaid is handled in Georgia is not the way it may be handled in North Carolina, Alabama, or Florida. This means that much of the information consumers have heard about Medicaid is incorrect.

Different Kinds of Medicaid

There are two different Medicaid programs seniors may be eligible for, the Community Care Services Program, and nursing homes.

Community Care Services Program

Seniors understandably want to stay in their own homes as long as possible, and the goal of the Community Care Services Program is to help folks do just that instead of moving to a nursing home.

Because nursing homes are so expensive, the State of Georgia wants to keep you out of them if at all possible. If you're already there, the state wants to see if it can take care of you in your home, the home of a caregiver, or in a community-based location so you can leave the nursing home for as long as possible.

People who qualify for the community care program are elderly and/or functionally impaired, and must be eligible for Medicaid and have to:

- qualify for the level of care provided by a nursing home;

- have limitations that make it difficult for them to perform normal daily living activities and live independently; and

- have health needs that can be met in the community with services offered by the program and within established individual cost guidelines. The individual cost is estimated based on the projected care plan.

These programs may provide assistance with bathing, dressing, some household chores, and other essential tasks. This may also provide relief for spouses who are caregivers.

Nursing Homes

The nursing home program is pretty much what it sounds like. It will pay for your care in a nursing home when you're no longer able to take care of yourself.

If you can no longer perform certain skills that you have to do every day to care of yourself, you may qualify, assuming you meet other qualification criteria.

If you cannot perform a number of activities of daily living (ADLs), you may need nursing home care.

Paying for Your Care

How are you going to pay for your care? Where is the money going to come from? Do you have the resources to pay for your care? Do you have long-term care insurance? Will you qualify for the Medicaid program?

Tough questions. You should begin thinking about this, and make plans, take action, *before* you need care, not after you need it.

Goal: Understanding the Importance of Long-Term Care Insurance: Don't Turn Up Your Nose Just Yet!

Why Consider Insurance?

We buy insurance for all kinds of risks. We buy insurance to transfer the risk of paying for an event to someone else, an insurance company.

Most of the risks we insure against actually have relatively low probabilities of causing us much out-of-pocket costs at all, much less a substantial amount. How many people do you know who have had their houses burn down or their cars totaled? Not that many, considering how many people you know.

Disability, however, is something different. We all stand a very great chance of becoming physically or mentally disabled, and this is even when you look at all age groups. If you consider senior citizens alone, they have a very high risk of physical or mental disability.

Is it a risk worth insuring? Compared to your regularly purchased auto or home policy, it certainly is.

What is Long-Term Care Insurance?

Long-term care insurance provides money to pay for care in the event you're no longer able to take care of yourself. Different policies give you this money in different ways. Some policies have a daily benefit, others have a monthly benefit, and still others have a pot of money.

Policies can be customized to pay for in-home care and/or nursing home care. This is where the policies become very interesting and potentially very valuable.

Our Goal:
Stay Home as Long as Possible

Though every senior wants to stay in his or her home as long as possible, the problem is that the other spouse, usually the wife, gets worn down, burns out, and ends up not being able to handle the job anymore. Think about it—how long will your wife be physically able to heft you around the house before she hurts herself or simply wears out? Not for very long. Unless she has help.

This is where long-term care insurance can come in; it can make it possible for you to hire caregivers who can provide better and more around-the-clock care for you while giving your wife a much-needed break.

With such home assistance, you may be able to stay at home for a longer time before you're forced to move to a nursing home. It may even enable you to never have to go to a nursing home. A lot of seniors like this plan.

Long-Term Care Insurance and Medicaid Planning

What is the best way to deal with long-term care issues? The answer depends on your particular circumstances, but one option to consider is to do two things at once.

One strategy is to do Medicaid planning and also getting long-term care insurance; the two can go hand in hand and allow you to stay in your home until you become eligible for Medicaid.

This combination strategy is a very powerful one that may actually save you lots of money as well as giving you more options and allowing you to stay in your home longer.

Medicaid Planning

Medicaid planning involves conducting a very complete, in-depth analysis of your financial and other circumstances to see what actions, if any, can be taken to make you eligible for Medicaid benefits immediately or in the future.

Myths and inaccuracies abound, however, regarding Medicaid planning, and two different, sad scenarios can come up. The first is that many people assume they could never qualify for Medicaid benefits, but they're incorrect about that. The second scenario is that many people think that qualifying for Medicaid is as simple as giving away all your assets to their children.

Don't Disqualify Yourself from Medicaid

Many people take the wrong kinds of actions in the mistaken belief they will be helping themselves qualify for Medicaid. In reality, they can easily, although unknowingly, ensure that they will not qualify for Medicaid for a long time.

Make no mistake—when it comes to Medicaid planning, it's not a time to "guess" what you need to do. You shouldn't rely on something friends told you at the beauty shop or grocery store that seemed to work out perfectly for them. The odds are very high that certain facts came into play in their situations that dramatically affected how their situations played out.

An experienced attorney will need very detailed information about your situation and review and analyze it to properly begin the Medicaid planning process. The analysis should take into account all the applicable federal and Georgia Medicaid laws and regulations as well as the "unofficial" ways the program is run daily.

Don't Give Assets Away! Speak with a Qualified Attorney

Most people are not aware of the Deficit Reduction Act of 2005 (DRA); it was passed by Congress as a cost-savings measure for Medicaid. The interplay between the DRA and Medicaid is very important. The DRA made some serious changes to the way the government looks at gifts and asset transfers that seniors make to their family members. In effect, the law will penalize seniors who give money or assets away regardless of the reason for the gift. The government assumes, rightly or wrongly, that the reason for the gift was to allow the seniors to make themselves eligible for Medicaid benefits.

Through the DRA, the government has created a system that severely penalizes Medicaid applicants who have not done their preplanning properly; it can prevent them from receiving Medicaid benefits for a period of time. That period of ineligibility will be calculated by looking at how much assets or money has been given away, and the penalty period can go on for many years.

Seniors often confuse various parts of the Medicaid rules and perform self-help Medicaid planning that actually leaves them in worse shape than they would have been in if they had consulted with a qualified Medicaid attorney.

There's lots of money at stake, so this is not the time for do-it-yourself planning or relying on hearsay and rumors.

Preplan Before You Need Medicaid

Many strategies can be used to help someone become eligible for Medicaid, but it's always best to plan ahead rather than to wait. People may be able to save a great deal of money by planning ahead, but even so, most still wait until a loved one is on his or her way to a nursing home before they begin planning.

People are procrastinators; they put important tasks off until another day. You'd be wise to learn from their mistakes—preplan to get the best result possible.

Emergency (Crisis) Planning

If you've not done any preplanning for Medicaid eligibility and you've waited until you're about to go into a nursing home (or you're there already), you may still have great options.

Medicaid planning is so much more than merely a matter of transferring assets, but the problem is that most folks (including most estate planning attorneys) are ignorant of the rules and regulations that apply to such asset transfers.

There are many different options when it comes to Medicaid planning, and each person's case is very fact specific. It's beyond the scope of this book to get into the actual details of the different options and when they should be used. Suffice it here to say some options may work best when used alone, and some may work best in conjunction with other options. This calls for a proper evaluation of any one person's situation; this is the key to crisis planning, that time when important decisions have to be made quickly.

Emotional Costs
of Caregiving on Families

- Mental stress on family caregivers

- Physical stress on family caregivers

- Financial stress on family caregivers who have to stop work, switch jobs, or work part time

- Loss of time for family caregivers

- Loss of freedom for family caregivers

- Conflicts caregivers have with their spouses

- Squabbles among your own children

Documents Your Family
Needs to Know About Before You Die

Save your family hours of stress and worry by having these documents in a place where they can be easily found.

Estate Planning

- will or living trust

- any other trust documents

- letters of instructions

- financial power of attorney

- medical power of attorney

Proof of Owership

- house and land deeds

- mortgages (contracts, escrow accoutns, balances)

- vehicle titles

- business ownership documents

- life insurance policies

- recent peronal and business tax returnes

Bank accounts

- list of accounts

- lists of any online passwords for accounts

- list and key for safe deposit boxes

Investments

- statements for brokerage accounts

- stocks and bonds certificates

- annuity policies

- money market account information

- CDs

- 401(k)

- IRAs

- pensions

Glossary

Accounting (in probate)

When an executor or administrator submits a detailed document that shows all the money and assets received and all disbursements and transfers to the estate's creditors and beneficiaries.

Administrator

The person given authority by the probate court by virtue of letters of administration to act on behalf of the estate.

Advance Directive for Health Care

A document comprising multiple parts used to select a health care agent, health care treatment preferences, and a guardian you would like the probate court to appoint for you if the court finds the person suitable. This document is an improvement over the older living will document.

Affidavit

A statement taken under oath and signed before a notary or other authorized person.

Asset Protection Trust

A trust designed to keep assets safe from creditors. This type of trust must be created and funded after taking into consideration the circumstances of the settlor's life or business.

Audit

A complete review by the probate court staff of the annual returns and supporting documentation filed by conservators.

Beneficiary

The designated recipient of a benefit under a will or contract or trust

Bond

The obligation of another to guarantee the proper performance of a duty and to pay any loss caused by the failure to so perform; in guardianship law, a guarantor, called a "surety," agrees to pay any loss suffered if a guardian or conservator fails to properly perform the duties of the office (mismanagement, loss through neglect, misappropriation, theft, etc.)

Capacity (to make a will)

A person's mental capacity can be impaired to differing degrees. A judgment will be made by the estate planning attorney that the person desiring to plan an estate has a good understanding of what he or she is doing in the estate planning process, its ramifications, what is being given away, and to whom it is going.

Caveat Proceeding

The filing if a formal challenge to the probating of a will in the probate court. The caveat may be based on many grounds, including a claim that the testator was unduly influenced, or didn't have the required degree of mental capacity, or fraud, or mistake. A caveat of sorts can be initiated simply by refusing to cooperate with the probate process, which may cause delay and cost, and cause the propounder of the will to file a court motion. For these reasons among others, a living trust (revocable trust) is attractive to some people and favored by some estate planning attorneys.

Child's Trust

A trust established to preserve assets for a beneficiary who may be too young, immature, or inexperienced in handling them. Such a trust can give the trustee discretion when it comes to giving assets to the trustee based on when the trust allows distributions to be made.

Codicil

A document to amend, change, or correct a will. The document must have the same signing formalities as a will requires. Using a codicil to amend or change a will compounds the issues of having to find the most recent version of the will and properly revoking any prior wills. The better practice is to revoke the prior will and create another will document.

Contingent Trust

A trust ready to spring into use if certain criteria happen or haven't happened, for example, minor children not reaching the age of majority (eighteen) before their parents are dead. The trust could still be put into force if it calls for assets to be managed on behalf of the child until the child turns twenty-five or thirty for example.

Discretionary Trust (see also Pot Trust

A trust established to fulfill the goal of preserving assets for a beneficiary, perhaps when the beneficiary is immature, doesn't have ability to manage money, or is inexperienced in life. The trustee may not be required to give out a certain amount or percentage of assets to the beneficiary at a certain age or life event; rather, the trustee has discretion to give assets to the beneficiary on an irregular basis based on when the trust allows distributions.

Durable Power of Attorney for Health Care

A document used prior to the creation of the Advanced Directive for Health Care document, which is no longer in use.

Dynasty Trust (see also Grandchildren's Trust)

A trust designed to bypass the children of the trust maker for the direct benefit of grandchildren; a trust designed with the anticipation that some of the trust assets will be left over to benefit grandchildren.

Estate

Everything a person has a whole or partial legal ownership interest in at the time of death. Examples include real estate, life estates, personal property, equipment, vehicles, investments, bank accounts, businesses, rights to royalties, mineral rights, patents, and copyrights.

Estate Administration

The process of requesting the probate court to issue letters testamentary or letters of administration so the executor or administrator can begin paying out a year's support if appropriate, paying any debts of the estate, and distributing the bequests to the beneficiaries. Other duties in the administration may include submitting an accounting to the court.

Estate Planning

The thoughts and actions involved in thinking through the various components of planning for the latter portion of one's life, including planning for mental or physical incapacity as well as how your assets will be divided. It is also concerned with protecting those assets during your life and also once they are given to your beneficiaries so they aren't lost to creditors or predators and will be able to serve the good of your children and grandchildren.

Execution, with required formalities (of will or trust)

The formal name of the process of properly signing and witnessing an estate planning document.

Executor or Executrix

The person chosen by the deceased, the testator, to distribute assets as called for under the will. The executor has no authority to take any action or distribute any assets until he or she has received the proper authority from the probate court.

Grandchildren's Trust (see also Dynasty Trust)

A trust designed to bypass the children of the trust maker for the direct benefit of grandchildren; a trust designed with the anticipation that some of the trust assets will be left over to benefit grandchildren.

Guardian (for adult)

The person appointed by the probate court to make decisions on behalf of the mentally incapacitated person (the ward). Financial decisions are made by the person the court appoints to be the conservator, who may also be the guardian.

Guardian (for minor children)

The person(s) listed in estate planning documents as the person the deceased wanted appointed to provide care for minor children.

Incentive Trust

A trust designed to reward a trust beneficiary for accomplishing certain goals, such attending college or technical school, holding a job, or some other worthy goal. The trust will also act as a disincentive for the beneficiary to not drop out of college or leave jobs after a short time.

Insurance Trust

A trust designed to receive life insurance benefits so the beneficiary doesn't receive the proceeds in a lump sum if they are inexperienced in money management or irresponsible or at risk of creditor lawsuit or divorce.

Intestate (Intestacy)

The term used to describe the situation in which someone dies without a will or if the will is unable to be found.

The probate court follows Georgia law in determining how to distribute the deceased's estate, which may be contrary to the way the deceased would have wanted his estate distributed.

Irrevocable Trust

A trust that can be compared to a box with a closed lid on it. Once an asset is placed in the trust, it cannot be removed by the person placing it in the trust. The giving of the asset cannot be "revoked." Compare this type of trust with a revocable trust, with which any asset in it can be withdrawn, and thus transfer can be revoked.

Joint Tenancy (Co-Ownership)

Used here to denote any form of co-ownership, including joint tenancy ownership of bank or investment accounts and real property. This type of ownership nullifies components of a deceased person's estate planning; it may also make certain assets vulnerable to creditors or lawsuits while the owner is alive.

Joint Will

A will for two people in one document instead of two documents. This is usually created for a married couple; the property is bequeathed to the surviving spouse and then to their mutual children. This is not the best way to create wills for a married couple; it is best to create two wills that will be probated separately.

Letters of Administration

The document given by the probate court to the person they appoint to act on behalf of the estate of someone who dies without a will. The letters of administration are issued by the court after a petition has been filed.

Letters Testamentary

The document given by the probate court judge to the executor allowing the executor to pay the estate's debts and distribute its assets. The letters are issued after a petition has been filed on behalf of the deceased person's estate and the submission of the deceased's last will.

Life Estate

The legal interest that remains after an owner gives away or sells all their rights to a piece of property except the right to use it during his or her life. They may also have the right to give or sell the life interest to a third party.

Living Trust (see Revocable Trust)

A legal document that acts as an open box of sorts into which assets can be put and also withdrawn. This open box allows the trustmaker lots of flexibility in the management of assets while still avoiding probate. It also allows the assets to be managed after death for the protection of children or grandchildren against creditors, bad marriages, bad money management, or irresponsibility.

Living Will

A document that directs your agent to make health care decision on your behalf should you be unable to do so. This document is much more rudimentary than the newer Georgia Advance Directive for Health Care, which allows for much more refinement in the selection of treatment preferences.

Medicaid

A federal and state program administered and partially paid for by individual states. The program is means tested; it is based on a person's income and assets. It can pay for medical treatment and home assistance or nursing home care for a person who meets certain age requirements.

Medicaid Planning

Arranging your income, expenses, assets, and liabilities to become eligible for public benefits under Medicaid. This is usually done by senior citizens so their assets won't have to be spent on long-term health care expenses but can be passed to their heirs.

Medicaid Trust (see also Nursing Home Trust)

Any trust that is a part of Medicaid planning to protect assets so they won't have to be expended for long-term care or nursing home expenses.

Minor Trust (see also Trust for Children)

A trust, usually established by parents, for minor children so they won't receive lump-sum inheritances when they reach age eighteen. Oftentimes, the goal of such a trust is to allow children to develop in responsibility while protecting them from financial hardship.

Non-Probate Assets

Assets that don't pass through probate to transfer ownership. This may have unintended negative consequences due to these assets not passing according to the will. Accidental disinheritance can result as well as unnecessary exposure of assets to creditors, divorce, or other issues heirs may have.

Nursing Home Trust (see also Medicaid Trust)

Any trust set up as part of Medicaid planning to protect assets so they won't have to be expended for long-term care or nursing home expenses.

Out-of-State Will (or Foreign Will)

A will created in another state of a person who was domiciled in another state at the time of death but who owned property in Georgia. The will must meet all the formalities of a will created in Georgia to be valid under Georgia law.

Pot Trust (see also Discretionary Trust, Child's Trust)

A trust established to preserve assets for a beneficiary who may be too young, immature, or inexperienced in handling them. Such a trust can give the trustee discretion when it comes to giving assets to the trustee based on when the trust allows distributions to be made.

Power Of Attorney (Financial)

A document that gives authority to one person to make financial decisions on behalf of another. The authority can be limited or unlimited. The authority can also be "springing"; it can grant such powers right after signing, or it can go into effect after the person becomes mentally incapacitated.

Probate

The process whereby the will of a deceased person is deemed to be the deceased person's true and correct will. An executor is given authority by the court to pay the debts of the estate and distribute the assets as called for by the will.

Probate Avoidance Trust (see also Living Will and Revocable Trust)

A trust designed to avoid the costs and time delays associated with the transfer of assets through the probate court process.

Residuary Clause

A clause in a will that sets forth what's to happen to assets the testator had when he died that weren't designated to a beneficiary or that were designated to a beneficiary who has since died. Without this clause, any assets would have to be dealt with using the laws of intestacy and would be treated by the courts as if a will didn't exist, at least as far as those particular assets are concerned.

Revocable Trust

A legal document that acts as an open box into which assets can be titled but also withdrawn. A revocable trust allows the trust maker much flexibility in managing assets while avoiding probate. It also allows the assets to be managed after death for the protection of children or grandchildren against creditors, bad marriages, bad money management, or irresponsibility.

Spendthrift Trust

A trust designed for assets meant to go to a beneficiary who is financially irresponsible. This trust will control when the beneficiary gets the assets and how much at a given time. The goal is to protect the beneficiary from himself or herself and preserve the assets so they can help the beneficiary for as long as possible.

Sprinkle Trust, aka Spray Trust (see also Discretionary Trust, Pot Trust)

A trust established to preserve assets for a beneficiary who may be too young, immature, or inexperienced in handling them. Such a trust can give the trustee discretion when it comes to giving assets to the trustee based on when the trust allows distributions to be made.

Testamentary Trust

A trust written during a person's life and contained in that person's will that comes into force only upon the testator's (the trustor's) death.

Trust

A legal document that consists of certain components, including the trustor (the maker of the trust), the trustee (the person who will carry out the specified reason for the trust), the beneficiaries (those who are to receive the benefits of the trust), the assets, and the document's clauses that set out the purpose of the arrangement. A trust can be either *inter vivos* (in force during the life of the trust maker) or testamentary (placed in the trust maker's will and coming into force only when the trust maker dies).

Trustee

The person or entity (can be a trustee company, a bank, or an investment firm) selected to have the responsibility of carrying out the precepts of a trust.

Will

A written document that sets out how the maker of the will (testator) requires assets to be distributed upon the death of the testator. The document may also set out the details of burial wishes.

Additional Reading

Beyond the Grave, Gerald M. Condon, Esq. and Jeffrey L. Condon, Esq.

The Complete Book of Trusts, Martin M. Shenkman, CPA, MBA, JD

Guide to Wills and Estates, The American Bar Association

Leave Your House in Order, John G. Watts

Love, Money, Control, Reinventing Estate Planning, Robert A. Esperti, Renno L. Petterson, W. Vito Lanuti, and Danniel J. Wexler

Splitting Heirs, Ron Blue, with Jeremy White

Wills and Administration in Georgia, Mary F. Radford, Professor of Law, Georgia State University College of Law

Wills and Trusts in a Nutshell, Robert L. Mennell, Professor of Law Emeritus, and Sherri L. Burr, Dickson Professor of Law, University of Mexico

Wills, Trusts and Estates, Gerry W. Beyer, Professor of Law, Texas Tech University School of Law

You and Your Aging Parents, The American Bar Association

About the Author

Attorney Jeff Fouts' family has been living in North Georgia since 1860. Jeff and his wife, Laura, have two children, Eden and Alex.

Jeff is a member in good standing of the State Bar of Georgia (since 1993), the Atlanta Bar Association, and the American Academy of Estate Planning Attorneys.

After graduating from the University of Georgia with a Bachelor's degree in political science, Jeff earned his Doctor of Law degree (J.D.).

In 1998, Jeff founded Retirement Planning Specialists, Inc., which is a Registered Investment Advisory firm. Jeff holds a Series 65 Securities License (Investment Advisor Representative), as well as a life insurance license.

He has served clients in all fifty states, as well as twenty-nine foreign countries. He has been admitted to:

- U.S. Supreme Court
- U.S. Tax Court
- U.S. Federal District Court, Northern District of Georgia
- U.S. Bankruptcy Court, Northern District of Georgia
- Supreme Court of Georgia
- Georgia Court of Appeals
- All Georgia courts, including probate courts

When not working on his clients' behalf, Jeff enjoys reading, walking, shooting sports, and camping.

WA